Community Care
Practice Handbooks

General Editor: Martin Davies

Residential Care: A Community Resource

Community Care
Practice Handbooks

General Editor: Martin Davies

Residential Care: A Community Resource

Leonard Davis

HEINEMANN EDUCATIONAL BOOKS
LONDON

Heinemann Educational Books Ltd
22 Bedford Square, London WC1B 3HH
LONDON EDINBURGH MELBOURNE AUCKLAND
HONG KONG SINGAPORE KUALA LUMPUR NEW DELHI
IBADAN NAIROBI JOHANNESBURG
EXETER (NH) KINGSTON PORT OF SPAIN

British Library Cataloguing in Publication Data

Davis, Leonard
    Residential care.—(Community care practice
    handbooks; 8)
    1.   Institutional care
    I.   Title   II. Series
    361'.05   HV59

ISBN 0 435 82264 0

Phototypesetting by Georgia Origination, Liverpool
Printed in Great Britain by Biddles Ltd, Guildford, Surrey

To my parents, Frank and Hilda Davis

Frank

Contents

Acknowledgements

For some years I have been contributing to social work journals, and the editors of *The British Journal of Social Work*, *The Community Homes Gazette* and *Social Work Today* have generously allowed me to draw on previously published articles in developing some of the themes in this book. These include 'Feelings and emotions in residential settings: the individual experience' (1977, *The British Journal of Social Work*, vol. 7, no. 1); 'Senses and sensibility' (1980, *The Community Homes Gazette*, vol. 74, no. 1, and reprinted, 1981, in *New Growth*, vol. 1, no. 1); and various short pieces from the In Residence page of *Social Work Today*; see list under 'Additional references' on page 116.

I am also grateful to Barbara Dockar-Drysdale, and to her publishers, the Longman Group Limited, for permission to adapt a section of her book, *Consultation in Child Care*, published in 1973. The Director of Durham Social Services, Peter Trietline, has allowed me to reproduce a section from Durham County Council's *Guide for Children in Care*.

The Inspectorate of the Inner London Education Authority produced a slim volume in 1977 entitled *Keeping the School under Review*. This provides helpful guidelines for looking at the work of a school. The Chief Inspector (Schools), Inner London Education Authority, Trevor Jaggar, has kindly allowed me to make use of some of the subject areas and questions in this booklet as a basis for the review of residential establishments set out in the Appendix.

Several people have given permission for me to include confidential material as case illustrations. For obvious reasons, they must remain anonymous. I am, however, able to acknowledge the help given by Graham Marsh, Director of Social Services, Buckinghamshire County Council, in allowing me to use a review which was undertaken in an old people's home in Buckinghamshire. All case material has been subjected to social disguise, and the names in the book are fictitious.

Peter Righton, formerly Director of Social Work Studies at the National Institute for Social Work, willingly read the draft manuscript, and made many valuable suggestions.

JUNE 1981   LEONARD DAVIS

1 The Legacy of the Past

Knowing few children of my own age,
I envied the children of literature
to whom interesting things were
always happening: 'Oliver Twist
was so *lucky* to live in a fascinating
orphanage!' (*Hons and Rebels*, Ch. 3)

Jessica Mitford

In most homes for elderly people, community homes, observation and assessment centres, residential schools, homes for mentally or physically handicapped people and hostels, even in new
purpose-built ones, we find links with the institutionalisation of
another era. Practitioners and administrators will have little difficulty in recognising these in their establishments, many of which
persist despite our efforts to develop alternative approaches to
group living, and to the care and control of those unable to live in a
house, flat or room, on their own or with friends or family. In
some instances staff have all but eradicated the legacy of the past.
In others the roots are deeply embedded and defy the attempts of
heads and managers of homes or members of staff to dig them out.
In a few homes there exists an apparent inability or unwillingness to
break into entrenched positions, staff and residents being caught
up in modes of care which thinly disguise the worst aspects of the
charitable, welfare, hospital, religious and unnecessarily custodial
antecedents of residential social work.

Of course, many people, young and old, have not only survived
but thriven on the experiences offered by skilled workers in caring
environments, and it is important that we should retain and
develop what has come to be recognised as good practice. I am convinced, however, that we should reject absolutely the innumerable
stigmatising elements of residential care that remain: firstly because
they are left over from a period in our history when we knew no
better, and secondly because they are now getting in the way of the
social work task, the elements of which are outlined in Chapter 3.
The creation of institutionalised residents is partly the result of our
own actions. Practitioners and administrators need constantly to
examine and re-examine how they are contributing to this.

Accommodation

What have we inherited? Geographically, many homes and residential schools are not well placed. Intent upon segregation our predecessors sited institutions away from the mainstream of life, most former approved schools, for example, being found in rural areas. Handicapped and elderly people, too, were often accommodated in large houses standing in their own grounds so that a walk up the long drive became a major expedition, if not an impossibility. Post-war building programmes failed to correct this. Local authority and voluntary homes are sometimes to be found in the least popular and the most inaccessible districts, near motorways, gasworks or factories. In contrast, I recently visited a comparatively new home for elderly people which offers shopping facilities close at hand and is comfortably located adjacent to a primary school where the colour, movement and daily rhythm provided by the comings and goings of the children for 40 weeks of the year lessen the feeling of insularity associated with living collectively in a large building.

Residential care has always been about living in large buildings, and many of these we have grown up with, sometimes ingeniously making them into smaller units. What it becomes difficult to excuse is a new building constructed for 50 residents living in one group, or adaptations to community homes which perpetuate units with 20 to 25 places when all our research points to the value of much smaller groups, sharing communal facilities as necessary.

Sexual segregation

The tradition of single sex establishments dies hard. Few community homes with education on the premises (CHEs) and residential special schools admit both boys and girls, although such segregation of the sexes seems increasingly unnatural and ill-advised in thinking about the healthy development of interpersonal relationships. The imbalance between male and female staff in male and female establishments is striking, with age-old fears and taboos as strong as ever. The physical and attitudinal constraints on adults making their own decisions about marriage or cohabitation and the development of heterosexual or homosexual relationships also reflect the often outdated preoccupations of care givers with over-protecting residents, or with over-controlling them. The opportunity and the right to freedom of choice in expressing their sexuality are determined by others merely because they live in residential settings, and in a way which is out of step with the social and sexual climate of the 1980s.

Mental handicap

One area of rejection for which we must accept responsibility is the residential care of mentally handicapped children and adults, and some people who are mentally ill. Thousands of these are not sick and have no place in a hospital setting. Above all, they are socially, mentally or physically inadequate, need compensatory social care and, in some instances, medical support. They have as much right to live in small units within the community as other deprived, neglected or handicapped members of our society. It so happens that they are sometimes less attractive to work with. However, within the limits of their potential they respond developmentally as much as other people, given an encouraging environment, a high staff ratio and intensive care of the order we decide to give to certain other resident groups. It feels morally indefensible to be selective in this way, and to commit some children to spending the rest of their lives in a hospital ward for 30 patients with minimum adult attention and denied access to the amount of physical contact and expressions of love which are their right. As much as any others, they remain the community's children, and the community's responsibility.

The language of residential care

The titles and names we use within residential care are important, and many have outlived their usefulness. Any edition of a social work journal will contain, for example, advertisements for a *superintendent* of a hostel for adolescent girls, a *deputy matron* of a children's home and a *deputy superintendent* of a home for elderly people. The words *houseparent, housewarden* and *supervisor* still appear, and at least one voluntary society permits the continued use of the title *sister*. Children cared for by 'sister' must be hard pressed to explain to their friends at school their biological affinity to the person who looks after them. The words 'superintendent' and 'matron' conjure up a particular image of custodial, medical or poor law type care. Children, teachers, employers, other agencies and the police all pick up the words, investing in them whatever connotations of power, authority, charity or sickness they choose. Even 'officer in charge' in the title of somebody running a home gives a strong feeling of rank, 'officers' and 'members', of course, forming the backbone of local authority organisation and management.

'Head of home' is, to my mind, the most acceptable title at present in use. For other members of staff the terms group worker, senior group worker and principal group worker if necessary seem the best we have to describe the job to be tackled, even if sometimes we may be a little embarrassed about the few skills provided in training for this to be approached with confidence. And we must remember that group workers have equal responsibility and equal licence to work with individuals. These comparatively neutral titles, together with the maximum use of Christian or given names (respecting the elderly person's wish to be known as 'Mr' or 'Mrs'), and the avoidance of 'Sir' and 'Miss' in young people's establishments will contribute towards a more natural framework for living together. Children should no longer be expected or encouraged to refer to their care givers in residential homes as 'aunt and uncle' or 'mum and dad', the former being surprisingly common and the latter not unknown. Some titles must make no sense at all to young children. 'Aunty matron' is one of the strangest I have come across.

Few people take sufficient notice of the language they use in residential social work, and indeed throughout welfare provision. While professional shorthand and a professional language seem inevitable in discussion among care givers I find it sad when residents, and especially young children, acquire an extensive institutional vocabulary, using words and phrases unknown to their families or their friends at school.

Throughout residential care children will ask: 'Are you on duty?' or worse 'Are you on?'; 'When are you off?' or 'Are you off?'; 'Are you sleeping in?'; 'When do you start your leave?'; and 'Are you doing the weekend?'. Specific language peculiarities are additionally found in most individual homes and schools. One CHE for girls has the following vocabulary, common to both staff and residents: *special supervision*, meaning that a young person stays in her night clothes, and is under the 24-hour surveillance of a member of staff who has no other responsibilities; *on ice*, meaning that a girl is not allowed out of staff sight, the adult even remaining outside the toilet as needs arise; *mobility ban*, meaning that no girl leaves the school unaccompanied; and *one to eight*, meaning that one adult may take out eight girls.

Special language moves beyond the boundaries of the residential establishment. Jean Lindsey suggests[1] that 'at home in care', a phrase running parallel to 'at home under supervision' should replace 'home on trial' because of its unfortunate associations, particularly for youngsters who have committed no offence. How right she is to point to one more legacy of the past that has no place in caring for children today.

Transport
There is the question of transport. In taking children and elderly or handicapped people on outings, for business or pleasure, I am concerned about the ease with which we use vehicles bearing the words 'London Borough of D—' or 'Y— County Council', with the appropriate coat of arms and painted in the same colours as the local dustcarts. Some residents come to accept this, in many ways as an extension of their institutionalisation. For others it hurts. Notice how pedestrians stop and stare at local authority coaches carrying groups of young people or adults, but do not give a second glance at similar vehicles painted in the manufacturers' standard colours. The use by social services departments of coaches and minibuses marked 'Ambulance' when the passengers are clearly not ill but handicapped and going about their daily affairs is further to be avoided. Recently I saw a crowded minibus with the words 'Hospital and Home for Incurables' painted in bold letters on each side.

One adolescent girl I knew preferred to walk any distance rather than ride in a council minibus in an area where she would be seen by her schoolfriends. I recall her saying: 'We might as well all wear badges with ''I belong to the London Borough of D—'' '. The provision of transport is, of course, most important, but so is the provision of unmarked vehicles.

Charitable organisations or local people raising funds for minibuses or coaches often expect to have the name of the establishment on the side of the vehicle, or worse 'Donated by XYZ'. One well-known entertainers' club is a particular offender in this respect. If such conditions are attached to gifts, I feel they should be refused, but on the whole people who are donating do respond to residents' needs if time is allowed to talk with them. Residential social workers have a duty to educate the general public and not to collude in making children, old people and institutions objects for charity. I appreciate the difficulties associated with anonymous giving and welcome neighbourhood involvement, but believe that no group of people should be closely identified with charity or welfare as they are driven around their local districts. Parading the dependence and inadequacy of the poor and needy is a phenomenon left over from the Middle Ages, and still observable in its purest form in the most traditional local authority or voluntary setting.

Elected members

Elected members, too, need a great deal of education. Perhaps intending members of social services committees should be prepared and trained in the same way as magistrates new to the bench. Some establishments have wall plaques to commemorate their inauguration by Councillor Mrs X or Councillor Mr Y. I feel that we should make every effort to have these removed. Is the sight of a written notice about living in a local authority assessment centre necessary every time a child passes through the front hall? What is the purpose of having a photograph of the chairman of the social services committee in the dining-room of an old people's home? There are sufficient other reminders of residents' 'in care' status.

We must avoid opening ceremonies and open days about two months after people have moved into a new home, refusing to indulge elected members' or committee members' needs to see the smiles on the faces of grateful residents, and to gain political capital from reports in local newspapers linking their names with good works. Providing opportunities for politicians, members, practitioners and administrators to view a new home before the admission of residents is, of course, a different matter and to be encouraged, as are well-planned visits for very small groups of people whose intention is to learn and not to look. Frankly, some members on rota visits (and the record of these needs careful checking if such visits have been established for any purpose) show such ignorance about the complexities of the work being undertaken that they cling pathetically to earlier vestiges of power and authority, asking for any complaints, signing the punishment and menu books, and inspecting the kitchen. What is really learned from reading a menu book?

Names of homes

There must be hundreds of homes named after trees or ending in the word 'field'. Some of the strangest names are dreamed up, or inherited and not changed, by social services committee members. Why not simply '52 Slough Road' or '23 Park Place'? These are less conspicuous, particularly if the home is going through a difficult phase and a young person has to give an address when seeking employment. Some names have the ring of local authority establishments and, for the teenager seeking a job in a department store, giving an address as 'The Willows' or 'Merryfield House' is not always the best recommendation. Even worse, councillors' names are still given to homes, as in the case of the opening of George Canning House in Birmingham in 1980.

Damaging practices

In the day-to-day practice of the art of residential social work (and I would see it more as an art than a science) we need to be more active in ferreting out the traits which mark the home as an institution, both in its internal procedures and in the way it operates across the boundaries and into the community, and which mark its residents as people apart. We cling to our inheritance partly because it is convenient for staff, and sometimes for residents in the short term; partly because it is difficult to escape from the fact that most homes and residential schools are firmly based in increasingly bureaucratic organisations; partly because of financial constraints; and partly because of the lack of space provided for lateral thinking in the face of pressures to respond to routine and crisis.

The list of potentially damaging practices is inexhaustible, different emphases and successes in overcoming them being found in each home. Some of my particular worries, all recently observed, are about rigid visiting times (stricter than the current hospital regulations from which the notion was originally taken); notices which demand that all visitors report to the office; the acceptance of second-hand gifts and toys at Christmas (possibly less worrying at other times of the year for general use, but not as personal presents); fund-raising activities by residents themselves for their own homes, that is, sponsored walks or raffles, instead of on behalf of a youth club they have joined or a charitable organisation they may be connected with; routine bathing on admission, and regularly on the same night of the week; compulsory viewing in a residential school of the early evening news on BBC television; special clothing for young people who have run away (shorts, nightdresses, pyjamas, dresses of a distinctive colour or, in the case of one CHE, just underclothes and a sheet taken from the bed); toilet paper marked 'Council Property' (invariably hard!); toilets without doors; plastic tableware and tumblers (where these cannot be justified); communal baths, that is, a number of unscreened baths standing side by side in a large room; the absence of tablecloths; all homes in a local authority having similar furniture, fittings and equipment; a far-too-early drink or supper snack which takes no account of individual preferences; the over-tight control of drinks and snacks between meals, especially in homes for young people where they often need to drink something other than water or to have a bite to eat; surgery parades; lining boys up naked for showers (strange, only boys?); on the insistence of rigid in-house hierarchies for decision making; clothing stores, except for a few attractive garments without other people's names for real emergencies; reliance on a sick bay; tea urns and large aluminium teapots (which, according to some elderly people, affect the taste of the tea); the absence of curtains in bedrooms and living-rooms; the tendency not to knock on residents' doors before entering their rooms; censored mail; tapped telephone calls; the routine recording of girls' periods, except for medical purposes, without the knowledge or agreement of the residents concerned; the ringing of aggressive-sounding bells at meal times (guaranteed to make youngsters boisterous and fearful of missing their share, and old people worried about being late); dormitory accommodation; cereal packets in plain wrappings (young children learn from reading the words and discussing over breakfast the pictures on a commercially-decorated cereal packet); visitors not offered tea and biscuits; visitors never able to join a resident for a meal; the regular public parade of all purchases by young people on their return from Saturday afternoon free time in the town (including personal items purchased by the girls, and much to their embarrassment) and having their value checked against the amount of pocket money given before leaving.

Trust

Many practices spell out 'I do not trust you' more powerfully than words. We can all accept these, or have to, outside our homes. When they pervade the nub of daily living it is time to resist. Voucher systems for obtaining clothing should, for example, be opposed. Young people have a right to buy their clothes from market stalls if they wish in the same way as their friends. Yes, there is a training element to be considered and sometimes, as part of this, we may adopt specific checking procedures for a short period with boys and girls who have difficulties in setting their own limits. Such devices are thus used to help children and not for administrative convenience. For young people to be clothed permanently on a voucher system whereby purchases are made from a limited range of stores is doing them a disservice.

As we shall see later, risk taking is essential in the development of any relationship, and in financial as in other matters there will inevitably be repercussions from time to time. Sometimes the money will go astray. I am not advocating the irresponsible distribution of large sums of money, but care practice demands the progressive trust of those being worked with, and trust with money is included in this.

It seems better than a 14-year old boy should mismanage £20 of local authority money, if this is used as a learning point, than in the first week at work he should take a similar amount from the till of his employer because never in his life has he had the feel of two £10 notes in his pocket. The experience of having in your possession and being trusted with a 'large' sum of money for the first time is one that adults forget when they become wage earners.

Corporal punishment
I find it difficult to believe that children and young people in residential homes and schools under the jurisdiction of local authority social services departments continue to be subjected to corporal punishment, and that otherwise seemingly caring professional workers allow themselves to become involved in such degrading practices. In different circumstances, similar aggressive and physically abusive acts would render adults liable to criminal proceedings, yet under what may only be described as the twisted ideas and ideologies of brutally-inclined members of social services committees, residential social workers co-operate in this retributive ritual. The professional associations seem weak in their opposition.

More than half the local authorities in England and Wales have now banned corporal punishment while others remain staunch advocates. For a while Nottinghamshire County Council appeared a particularly misguided local authority in this respect. Caning in its children's homes, abolished by Labour in 1974, was reintroduced when the Tories took control in 1977. Residential staff apparently accepted with little protest the new licence to beat young people with the result that in 1979 16 boys and one 15-year old girl were caned.[2] At first the meeting of the new Labour social services committee in May 1981 corporal punishment was again banned throughout children's establishments.

What does the adult, the paid professional adult appointed for his or her abilities to care for people in difficulties feel on inflicting physical punishment? Does it enhance his or her standing, not as head of the home or the deputy, but as a *person*? Will that same individual within the space of half an hour be offering physical comfort to a 10-year old girl upset by bullying from an older boy? Some parents would perhaps not wish to have such a worker ministering to their young daughter. Beating another person is by no means a neutral act. Some would say it can never be separated from sexual fantasies. There is evidence that pornography dealing with the details of caning children is a growth industry, and a willingness to beat an adolescent with a stick would, for my part, bring into question the overall worth of any worker.

The imposition of physical hurt by the adult on a child (we are only talking of a minority of practitioners) is a worrying and dangerous element in residential child care. Those caught up in the process must be helped to seek alternative support structures. My problem lies in including within one broad group of social work staff, ostensibly committed to the same caring ideals, two types of worker: those who, as fieldworkers, compile at risk registers and become particularly sensitive to weals and bruises, signs which may eventually lead to the removal of a child from a home; and those, perhaps from the same social services department, who as part of the residential assessment and caring programmes they are developing inflict similar or even more severe weals and bruises. Field social workers have equal knowledge of children's aggressive, destructive and unacceptable behaviour, yet have no part in corporal punishment. The few remaining practitioners who continue to favour the use of physical punishment as a disciplinary measure provide arguments for those who would wish to make unfavourable contrasts between residential social workers and their colleagues in the field.

Broader issues
In thinking about the legacy of the past there is undoubtedly a need to look not only at the detail of residential care but also at some of the broader issues, for example the relationships between the private, voluntary and public sectors; the value of community-based as opposed to rurally-based residential settings; and the meaning of success. The case of Merissa throws these dilemmas into relief.

Merissa was away from her home in Deptford and living in a country community for nearly five years, spending her holidays in a children's home from which she made brief visits to her mother and her cohabitee and their four children. The decision to send Merissa to X School was made at a case conference. Her mother was anxious, baffled and pleased to allow others to provide a solution. Merissa was an intelligent girl and settled well in the small local assessment centre during the six months she waited for a vacancy. She was admitted to X School two weeks after a half-day pre-placement visit.

I would suggest that this is not an unusual pattern for a young person in care. All seemed well. Despite some behaviour problems, Merissa's standards in matters of dress, conversation, artistic ability, hygiene and social skills made her a charming person and a delightful companion, apparently on the road to a career and a settled existence. At 16 years, Merissa suddenly gave up everything and returned home to face a culture of poverty and squalor in the terraced house in the condemned street which was to be her home over the next two years.

I knew Merissa well, and she often related the behaviour difficulties identified by staff in the therapeutic community to the continuous struggle with her conscience to square up what was happening to her with what was happening to her family. Eventually she was forced to abandon everything, and to share again. The change of climate was extreme, bewildering and overwhelming. Merissa turned to prostitution before being admitted as a voluntary patient to a psychiatric hospital two years later.

I was left with many questions, for example: economically, was a large sum of money spent to the best advantage for Merissa and her family? In human terms, what were we trying to accomplish? Was there ever hope of a real resolution to Merissa's almost inevitable difficulty of coping with the divorce from her earlier lifestyle without at the same time lifting the whole family materially and emotionally?

Occasionally, as a response to the needs of an individual it may be helpful for a person to live for a little while in a rural setting away from the conflicts he or she was unable to resolve in a town or city. Such time out, however, should be carefully monitored and be purposeful in direction, not occurring merely because of the inadequacy of local authority facilities. However enriching the sometimes lengthy experiences provided in an artificial country community, they may later become barriers to urban living and to the cut and thrust of social, work and family relationships, unless residents are enabled to remain in contact with the real world to which most must inevitably return.

Local authorities have always used outside agencies in providing residential care for their clients. They will continue to do so, and in the current political and economic climate, may need more and more to develop these contacts. A great deal of pioneering work in residential care, especially child care, has happened in the private and voluntary sector. In some instances they remain leaders in the field; in others the standards of care they offer fall well below those available in local authorities. Before social workers place residents in settings outside local authorities they should look much more closely – and critically – at what is being provided. The use of an establishment as a haven at a moment of crisis must be balanced with the long-term interests of the client. As in the case of Merissa, success may ultimately prove destructive.

Often we choose not to take responsibility for the events that follow decisions to point other people's lives in an entirely new direction. Frequently these decisions are made quite briskly and do not emerge from thinking gently with the person concerned about his or her own sense of direction. Surely the strongest indicator must come from within the individual.

The need to change attitudes

Residential staff should be professional workers developing attitudes, creating environments and upholding only those practices that will reduce the distance between the living styles of those in care and people living more or less successfully in their own homes. Their responsibilities include working towards the removal of regulations that conflict with their caring task. Given motivation, a forceful approach, a willingness to take risks and a desire to convince others (including colleagues) of the handicapping nature of so much that is taken for granted, many practices cost little to change, but have the potential for shaking off layers of stigma and frustrating administrative procedures. Shadows of the past linger stubbornly both inside our homes and residential schools, and over the politics, policies and machinery of local government of which staff and residents are component parts.

Some would argue that such a vision of residential care can never become a reality within the structure of local authority social services departments. I do not subscribe to this opinion. While it may be difficult, and while success may mean achieving 90 per cent of what I am advocating, our only course is to try. Some homes and residential schools I am familiar with come very near in their demonstrations of good practice.

What is our starting point? On the one hand, most of our residential provision is managed by local authorities, known principally for their need to control, for their petty administrative procedures and for their reluctance to change. Often they act, consciously or unconsciously, on a residual welfare model. On the other hand, we know that a person cannot 'live' in a bureaucracy, and that a child cannot be parented by an organisation. Somehow we have to bridge this gap. The initial steps must be taken by the staff themselves: firstly by making sure that they do not replicate in modified form within their own establishments the local authority structures they find so irksome in their parent body; secondly by looking again at their reasons for continuing to collude with some aspects of institutional living that are entirely their responsibility and often within their power and ability to change; and thirdly by convincing those outside residential communities that the work can only be lastingly beneficial to residents if staff are encouraged and enabled to set themselves free from earlier traditions, prejudices and ways of working.

These are formidable tasks for some homes and residential schools in many local authorities. Even within homes we find senior staff unprepared to think about these 'initial steps'. Local authorities as employers, and senior staff as managers, seem too frequently blind or deaf to the need to respond creatively to such initiatives. They have lost sight of or never had the resident's view of what it means to be 'in care'.

The seriousness of intervention

Intervention in the life of another person must always be taken seriously. Intervention resulting in the movement of that person away from his or her home and into a residential setting is likely to effect a change in the nature and direction of the individual's life in ways that are sometimes irreversible: an adolescent's bed may be taken over by a lodger; an elderly person may lose the tenancy of her flat; or a young handicapped child may become emotionally excluded from his family. In taking the decision to receive a person into residential care (I find the words 'receive' and 'reception' softer than 'admit' and 'admission' and will use the former in this text whenever referring directly to an individual client) we must offer both person and family some satisfaction that what is being provided as an alternative to living at home on a permanent basis or as a rehabilitative measure is qualitatively better than what went before. Without such an assurance we must surely question the right to intervene.

Often an elderly person, a family or an adolescent cries out for help in making sense of this unyielding world. Society's answer to its failure to make more than a palliative response to social injustice, the lack of domiciliary provision and housing ills is to panic and to put large numbers of its citizens into residential homes. Consequently over the last two decades we have built more and more establishments for more and more people now destined to live out a substantial part of their lives in settings unlikely to meet many of their primary needs.

The political dimension

I suspect that in the hearts and minds of many individuals moving into residential care and their families, there remains a feeling that economically and socially they have never had access to an equal share of our collective wealth or potential emotional well-being. A glance at the social class of any group of residents illustrates this point. For society and for residential social workers to ignore these feelings and then to translate this unfair distribution of material goods and the lack of opportunity for personal advancement into widespread individual and family pathology is to intensify the ills and the injustices to which residents have already been subjected. As a background to our work there is a political dimension that must be addressed, although in varying degrees by different practitioners. This political dimension may be tackled on several fronts, for example at the point about decisions for reception into care; in maximising resources to ensure appropriate levels of response to meet residents' needs; in making sure that residents retain their citizens' voice; and by ensuring the rights of residents.

For too long we have tolerated low standards where it matters most: in the quality of the service delivery at the level of the resident. For too long we have compromised in important areas of our work, thus giving to the resident less chance of overcoming the difficulties which brought about his or her movement into residential care, or of being given a really satisfying alternative to the life left behind. In a semi-structured home forming part of a large bureaucratic organisation and sometimes overburdened by the heavy demands of residents, colleagues, administrators and members, it is easy for residential social workers to lose sight of the political ideologies primarily responsible for many people needing residential care in the first place.

There is no need for residents to accept second best because of the wider political and economic decisions made at a great distance from their establishments. However loud they shout they will never get their fair share of the cake. So they must be encouraged and aided to make their wishes known, whether it is for transport for the home (because the local authority has chosen to build on a site far removed from the centre of the community); for individual rooms; for more frequent visits from fieldworkers; for greater participation in all meetings about them; or for full information about any 'treatment' to be given.

Our society is full of oppressed groups: black people, mentally handicapped people, those who are homosexual, people who are mentally ill, elderly people and children who by accident of birth or later change of circumstances do not live in 'respectable' nuclear families, together with all the minority groups who because of their differences make up isolated sections of the community. To be a member of one of these groups and to feel the stigma is bad enough; later to become a resident in a home puts an individual at the bottom of the pile.

I think that many definitions and examples of good practice over the last decade, while having many merits, have not in any way gone far enough in helping to liberate the people they are there to serve. Basically, residential care remains conservative, hierarchical, over-controlling and encapsulating, largely because it is practised in local authority social services departments displaying all the same characteristics. This need not necessarily remain so. We have no reason to transfer the same stifling concepts to the living experiences of large numbers of people, and new patterns of care are possible within local authorities.

Residential social workers must take steps to reverse residents' feelings of inadequacy, difference and inferiority in ways other than concentrating on the personal and family pathology referred to earlier. The obligation to remain politically aware, to remind others of their responsibilities and to work with colleagues and residents on every occasion to bring about change must become an essential part of the residential social workers' task. Residents must move from the role of passive recipients of services to active participants in the process of change: in their individual lives, in the life of the group or the home, and as members of the society to which they belong. It is against this background that the scenario for residential care in the 1980s and 1990s should be set.

2 Creating a Climate of Concern

Admission to a residential setting is surrounded by strong feelings of fear, relief, anger and anticipation mixed with unrealistic expectations or abject despair which may temporarily cloud the mind of a client entering the unknown. We pay insufficient attention to this phase. Residential social workers are familiar with their working environment. For a new resident it may be the first move away from home. In many instances the process will be painful. We may only be able to minimise this, but in so doing can lay the foundation for work with a new member of the group.

Failure in the community

Most people move into residential care because they have 'failed' in the community, have become nuisances in school or are scapegoated by the family, are thought to need protection and control or have been let down by society in the level of its domiciliary, day care or sheltered housing provision. The key word is 'failure' – by the individual, by the family, by the school or by the society we have created. Failure begets stress, aggression, rejection and depression, both in the individuals concerned and in those who surround them. Few people arrive on a ticket of hope, the pathway from home to residential establishment being variously strewn with threats, delinquent acts, violent quarrels, running away, alienation, bereavement, entrenched positions, a breakdown in communication, severely damaged relationships, loss, deteriorating faculties, unexpected handicap and unfulfilled promises.

Too often pride, the need for a brave face and the numbness associated with the event enable staff initially to ignore a great deal of this sea of stress and distress and to pack away the intensity of feeling with the same speed and tidiness as the drab suitcases carried in by their bewildered owners.

There is something sad about a person whose wordly possessions can be contained in a single suitcase, sadness that we are not always able to pick up, or willing to bear in the concentrated form found in a succession of newly-received residents. This may be our first mistake, pointing up as it does the seeming security of our own positions vis-à-vis the extreme insecurity of theirs. Everything – knowledge, power, freedom of movement and possessions – lies with the care givers. The child or adult moving from his or her own home and taking on the unaccustomed role of resident has to wrestle with the past, memories, confusions, regrets and anger. Sometimes he or she is confronted with a seemingly hostile group.

Outward calm and inner turmoil

The five people I am about to describe were all model residents during the first few months of their stay. Outwardly calm and conforming, they were inwardly bearing very heavy loads.

Fourteen-year old *Carol* arrived at the assessment centre dressed in school uniform and carrying a hockey stick. Her foster home placement had broken down after six reasonable and uneventful years with an earlier history of neglect and deprivation in her own home. During the first term of her third year at secondary school she had become unco-operative with her foster parents, disruptive at school and 'started to mix with the wrong sort'. Mr Gibson, her foster father, told the field social worker that he was worried about the effect of Carol's behaviour on his wife's health and asked for her removal. Only much later did it become known that the 17-year old son of Mr and Mrs Gibson had for some time been demanding sexual intercourse from Carol, holding over this comparatively unsophisticated girl the threat to tell any future boyfriend or husband that she had been a willing partner. Carol struggled with this alone, was unable to be critical to her foster parents about their son and experienced her emerging sexuality as unwelcome, destructive and intensely frightening.

Mrs Ashton had lived with her daughter and son-in-law since the death of her husband seven years previously. She occupied the large room over the garage. It was for the family a case of 'What shall we do with granny?'. Tales abounded about her depression, her threats of suicide, her odd behaviour, her unwillingness to leave her room and strained family relationships. Mrs Ashton was finally admitted to an old people's home when she started refusing to eat. Again, it was only revealed after many months where the problem was really centred. It transpired that her daughter and son-in-law's eldest son wanted to get married, his only hope as an unemployed builder's labourer and living in an already overcrowded house being the chance to take over his grandmother's room. Nobody in the family had discussed anything with the elderly lady, but she had overheard conversations and her physical presence had increasingly been seen by the remainder of the household as a stumbling block to the implementation of their plans. The secrecy of the family preyed on Mrs Ashton's mind, and the conspiracy to exclude her was sufficiently strong to drive her out. A proud and uncomplicated person, Mrs Ashton found it difficult to think badly of her daughter, son-in-law and grandson. She certainly could not discuss her worries outside the family.

Malcolm was a tall boy, over six feet in height and 17 years of age. He was mentally handicapped and had always lived with his parents and twin sister, Margaret. Margaret was of average intelligence. Over the summer period Malcolm had made a nuisance of himself in the local park, gaining a reputation as a 'flasher'. He was unconcerned and unrepentant, smiling wryly when reprimanded. With the co-operation of the police and various social work agencies no formal action was taken, but he took up residence in a hostel.

It came to light that Malcolm had been encouraged in his actions by younger boys on holiday from school who had egged him on and rewarded him with sweets and cigarettes for his performances. By nature quiet, friendly and home-loving, Malcolm contained within him a great deal of bewilderment and unexpressed anger about his removal from home, all of which went unnoticed when he moved into 84 Western Avenue.

Kevin was 13 years old, seriously delinquent, not immediately attractive to adults, and lived with his mother, father and two beautiful sisters. He disliked school and truanted. On coming into care Kevin presented as tough, just plain tough. His parents displayed considerable hostility towards him, and his father had beaten him on three occasions. Much later it was revealed that Kevin's sisters were unbelievably successful in everything they did at school, and that his own very minor achievements over the years in swimming and art had never been of any consequence to anybody. So he just gave up and joined a delinquent group. Kevin remained, however, deeply troubled by the emotional gulf that existed between him and his parents.

Following a car accident, in a vehicle driven by her husband, *Meg Johnson* spent a long time in hospital, had a series of operations and was then transferred to a convalescent home. Meg was paralysed from the waist downwards, but had nevertheless always anticipated a return home, the promise of domiciliary help and home nursing services having frequently been made to her.

There was no reason to expect anything different. The couple had enjoyed a happy marriage for 12 years. After the accident, Mr Johnson had cared well for their three children, aged 11, nine and five, for over a year, but eventually the strain began to tell and, on the advice of a friend, he employed an au pair, unbeknown to his wife. A relationship developed between Bill Johnson and Monique, the au pair. She became pregnant, was well accepted by the children and Meg was gradually squeezed out of the home, physically and emotionally. Guarded but often bitter reports were eventually relayed to Meg by both her parents and her husband's parents and, when visiting their mother, the children spoke freely of Monique who now looked after them and the new brother or sister they were to have.

As physically whole as she would ever be, Meg had to make a permanent home in a residential setting. When she moved in, the information about her was factual: about the accident, about her paralysed body, about her need for frequent nursing attention. Nobody knew the extent of Meg's inner conflicts.

Carol, Mrs Ashton, Malcolm, Kevin and Meg Johnson are not unusual residents. Between them they demonstrate a range of individual needs, a variety of life experiences and diversity in the pattern of desirable responses to be made by staff during the months ahead. Initially they needed to be received into facilitating environments. With all of them, to varying degrees, there was a social work task to be undertaken. This will be identified and developed in Chapter 3.

These residents were not abnormal people, they were not sick and they did not require treatment in the unfortunate sense still commonly used. In other circumstances they could have been my friends or your friends, my neighbours or your neighbours. Their worries and their regrets were to be found on the same continuum as yours or mine. It so happens that their capacities to cope, their personal networks and the strength gained from earlier experiences were insufficient to combat the crises in their lives. For different reasons they could no longer live at home. Their immediate need was for an alternative environment in which to live, to grow and to be understood.

Many traditional residential settings merely erode further the limited self-confidence felt by newly-arrived people. It is for that reason that I dwell at some length on the importance of creating a climate of concern. In this chapter we are thinking about attitudes which span the client groups and about some of the general principles underpinning our work. To my mind, they form the basis of a number of absolutes which individual practitioners should develop and be prepared to defend as a background to their work with individual residents or with groups. On many issues there should be no compromise.

The admission process

Every client being considered for a residential place has a right to at least one pre-admission visit. The onus must be on the social worker, field or residential, to give reasons for not arranging a preliminary visit, and these should be explained to the person and his or her family.

Written information about the establishment should be available to the client, to his or her relatives and to the field social worker involved. Every home should have a prospectus, and this should be updated frequently, perhaps twice a year, to allow for staff movements, changes in domestic arrangements or increases in allowances. Residents and their families have a right to know about the qualifications and experience of the people who will be looking after them and making far-reaching decisions about their lives. If, as local authority employers, we feel hesitant about this because in many cases we have no qualified staff or employ untrained agency staff, then this should be revealed, and the challenges of the clients and their families responded to. Politically, this could be powerful medicine.

Before admission, people have a right to know both about the restrictions which residential life may bring and about the new opportunities which they may expect: opportunities set out in the shape of a contract, not necessarily written, but one which means that their future is not at the whim of market forces that may be so crippling as to make a nonsense of the original admission agreement. Before moving in residents should be told about pocket money, clothing allowances, visiting arrangements, personal possessions, pets, medical facilities and future contacts with relatives and friends. In the space of a few days, or even hours, residents are moving from one world to another, perhaps from one set of values to another. Given enthusiasm, motivation and a clear mind, such changes are rarely accomplished without uncertainty and apprehension. Under the circumstances in which many people become residents it may be difficult to assess the upheaval to their physical and emotional beings.

There may be no ideal time of the week for moving into residence, and no ideal time of the day. Some factors, however, may be taken into consideration. On arrival, a person should be in immediate contact with a member of staff, or sometimes a responsible resident, who has time allocated and is able to offer a measure of continuity in the hours and days to follow. A choice of dishes should be offered at the first meal; pressures to join in group activities too soon should be avoided; and it should be remembered that the first day may be full of anxieties for a resident arriving early in the morning. Perhaps a mid-afternoon arrival is preferable. The week, too, may seem long when admission takes place on Monday; the silence of the preceding weekend may heighten tension and the following weekend may seem far away. It should be explained to the newly-received person that future contacts with family and friends will be arranged on an individual basis, and not on that of a magic number by which some establishments attempt to speed up the settling-in period, for instance, by rules stating that 'nobody goes home until they have been here a month'. This may very occasionally be appropriate. In other cases, it may be disastrous, increasing anxiety or precipitating running away.

Transfer and discharge
Transfer and discharge should be handled with similar care, and because staff have greater control over timing than at the point of admission, these should be at the best pace for each resident. Temptations and pressures for hurried discharges and transfers abound with too little recognition of the rate at which adjustment can be made from residential to independent living, from residential care to a foster home, or from a small unit to a residential school. The movement of a person from one environment to another is more than a paper transaction or an administrative telephone call. It is about getting beneath the surface of stress or outward composure and finding out the hidden fears and fantasies of residents. For example, these may relate to the distance from the new residential home to the school the child is already attending; to the type of people a resident will be living with; to concern about care at night; or to basic questions about bathing and toilet arrangements. We all find security in our ability to control large areas of our environment. Residents often have little control of their lives and their futures, and therefore cling desperately to whatever makes them feel safe.

On transfer particularly an important issue arises, namely, the way in which we go about a preliminary visit. And this concerns the fieldworker as much as the residential social worker. We may say to a resident: 'We are going along to the home at 57 Green Vale to see whether you like it' or 'We are going along to the home at 57 Green Vale to see it before you move in'. If in fact there is no choice, it is unfair to hide behind the 'to see whether you like it' formula. With a reluctant client, the use of the former may make the visit a much easier experience because of the thought that the home can be rejected if it does not come up to expectations. For the resident to learn later that the transfer is going ahead anyway shows dishonesty on the part of the worker.

When moving to a new establishment, a person should be told what the care givers know about him or her, what written information they have been given, who supplied this information, and what documentation is held in the home. The client should also know what is to be recorded during the stay, and what happens to files when residents leave the home. The shadow of a file, and its unknown contents, is a strong weapon in the hands of the power holders.

Some places keep no records at all; others have detailed comments on every aspect of the residents' behaviour, their moods, their relationships and their outside contacts. Again, I would suggest that the onus must be on the workers to justify the records they keep, and within these records to defend what is not shared with the resident. Sometimes these are difficult things to do.

Exchanging information

Between field and residential workers the flow of information is, for the most part, one-way. Monday mornings will often bring a spate of telephone calls from residential homes to area offices notifying fieldworkers of incidents: about a child who has run away (may we forever bury the words 'absconded' and 'absconder', especially when referring to a youngster?); or about a handicapped person who has been scalded or broken a limb. Rarely is the message put in writing. One reason is that few homes have secretarial help. On this issue, I find it hard to understand why fieldworkers have administrative and typing assistance while the majority of residential social workers are given no help except in the largest establishments. In this way a disproportionate amount of senior staff time is taken up with work that is essentially clerical, thereby drawing competent practitioners away from the developmental, teaching, enabling and monitoring aspects of their jobs for which they are primarily in post.

It would seem equally important for residential establishments – and residents also, as soon as convenient – to be informed of home visits by field social workers, so that they will know that a father has been gaoled, or a not-so-young daughter of an elderly resident has been admitted to hospital and will not be able to visit her mother. Each residential home, within the guidelines laid down by the particular local authority or voluntary organisation (assuming they all have them), will develop its own system of records and record-keeping. In a planned admission, there is need for written information before the resident arrives – and, as mentioned earlier, he or she should know that this is being given.

Reasons for admission

Social histories do have their place, but more important is the answer to the question 'Why now?', pointing to the problems making an impact at the present time. What is interfering with this child's education that brings about truancy, causes him to steal and makes him run away from home? What has arisen at this time between a daughter and her elderly mother which means that they no longer feel able to live together? What prevents a 16-year old physically handicapped girl from continuing to live at home? The 'here and now' of the breakdown or sudden, marked deterioration takes on an urgency that must be investigated immediately if there is to be any hope of rehabilitation or compromise arrangements during the next six months following reception into care, a period well known to provide the maximum chance of avoiding a long stay in a residential home. During this time a concerted effort is required by both field and residential staff.

It is no basis for a successful outcome if residential care is provided just because of the non-availability of more appropriate alternatives. Any examination of changes in a person's life which push others to request reception into residential care should lead to an exploration of other methods of providing support. There is no justification for receiving people into residential care on the sole basis of inadequate domiciliary services, sub-standard housing or financial hardship.

Sometimes, of course, residential care becomes the placement of choice where, for example, a young person cannot bear the prospect of any more family life, say with a violent step-father; where 24-hour seven-day-a-week care is essential (although even this should be provided at home whenever possible); or where an elderly person with previously strong family attachments prefers to take on a more dependent role as extreme old age approaches.

We also have to acknowledge that many people are forced into residential care against their will, sometimes by order of the court; by exhibiting such odd, destructive or aggressive behaviour that by the rules of our society intervention is demanded; or, in the case of a limited number of children, young people and adults, for their own protection.

On taking the decision to place an individual in residential care we need to be clear about several points, for example who is wielding the power that determines reception into care, what alternatives have been considered, what choice has the prospective resident, and in whose best interests reception into care is being requested or recommended. Reasoning, issues and responsibilities soon become blurred after a person has taken up a place in a residential unit, especially when no written statement is made about problems and plans.

Building identity

There is one further consideration when thinking about record-keeping. We should work harder with children, adolescents and adults who spend long periods of their lives in residential care at building personal histories. This may be done through a life story, and should be well illustrated. We all know the disappointment and anguish of a 14-year old who has no photograph of herself as a young child or even at 12 years of age. In later life she has no answer for her own child in response to the question: 'How did you look when you were young, mum?'. However sordid the past may be, it is better to share personal histories with young people on the earliest possible occasion, as a natural event as they grow up, so that doubts and perplexities that arise can be tackled. A personal history must never be a leaving present for a young adult as he or she goes out of care.

Elderly people, too, need parallel reinforcements of their self-images by having photographs taken, with sufficient copies for them to distribute to friends, relatives and care staff if they wish. The symbolic value of such gifts allows frail and elderly residents to feel that, by giving pictures of themselves, they are remaining in people's thoughts, have a tiny stake in the lives of others, and retain personal qualities and personal attractiveness that make them worth remembering. It might be valuable for every head of home to satisfy her or himself that all residents in the establishment have had their photographs taken at least once during the last year.

Critical points

There are a number of critical points for staff and residents during any 24-hour period, for example going to bed, getting up and meal-times. To these we may add some of the primary concerns of residents which often manifest themselves at these times, for instance regarding sleeping arrangements, the preparation and presentation of food, the use of the toilet and personal possessions. It is the potential mismatch between residents' needs and rights and staff anticipation and skill that makes these points critical.

The approach of bedtime brings a wave of strong feelings to certain people: the first time as an eight-year old sleeping alone in a single bed; changing to a smaller or larger room, perhaps with a high ceiling; the first time as a 12-year old sleeping in a room with physically stronger boys who earlier in the evening have threatened to 'beat you up'; adjusting to unfamiliar settling down routines; being frightened of sexual assault; or the first time as an 80-year old sleeping in a room with four others, one of whom wanders at night and appears dangerous, and another who moans eerily every few minutes.

To a young child the toilet may seem a long way down the corridor, the red bulb of the night light may produce weird shadows and the thought of passing the black entrances to nine or ten other rooms as he wends his way along the passage is enough to make him decide to spend the rest of the night in a wet bed. Not all establishments have the flexibility or facilities that allow residents to continue former habits, for example taking a hot drink to bed, reading until ready for sleep or listening to the radio. There may be certain demands made about nightclothes: females may be dissuaded from wearing flimsy garments, males may no longer be able to sleep in the nude. The slippery feel of rubber under the bottom sheet and a plastic covering over the pillow may be uncomfortable, until newly-arrived residents have proved that they are not enuretic.

I know of very few homes or residential schools that have evolved adequate systems of care designed to reduce the tensions of the individual during the hours of darkness. Some people are frightened at night: they fear physical attack; that their belongings will be damaged or stolen; that somebody will urinate in *their* bed; or that a room companion will start a fire with a lighted cigarette.

We all know of young children who, during the night, will almost involuntarily climb into the beds of siblings or other children in order to seek warmth or comfort. With older children and adults sexual excitement may become apparent as they prepare to sleep. The intimacy of group living is an experience that inevitably heightens sexual awareness. For adolescents particularly, the presence of members of the opposite sex in another wing of the building, or even only 18 inches away on the other side of a wall, may be overwhelming in its stimulation.

Some members of staff may still be worried by children who masturbate in bed, and it is common for reports to appear in their log books: 'Caught Jane "at it" again last night. Made her wash her hands'. Mutual masturbation, too, will occur. Viewed as a developmental phase, it is often appropriate to talk about this with the young people concerned, providing an opportunity to increase their understanding of biological needs, of the nature of physical and emotional attraction, and of socially acceptable conduct.

The reluctance to settle down quickly is a further indication of the feelings that emerge at this time. Sometimes this reflects residents' dissatisfaction with their share of staff attention in the preparations for bed. Favourite hot drinks, hot water bottles, cuddly toys (these should be universally available, even for older children and some adults) and time for unhurried conversation will induce sleep and anticipate the fears of the night.

Some hostels for mentally handicapped men and women now permit a male and a female to share a room if they wish. The provision of single beds, however, may give a contradictory message. Within the context of growing affection, and well supported by care staff, there is no reason why mentally handicapped adults should be prevented from living together and sharing their lives to the full. Many do show responsibility in a warm, secure environment.

If, in residential settings, we are working with people at a level of understanding that aims to enhance their whole life experience, then it seems right to think a little more about the third of the week when we are least likely to be in touch with their inner worlds. The simplest – though not the wisest – course is to observe, record and sometimes punish the irregularities and misdemeanours of the night, and not to work with them in the same way that we approach daytime disturbances. The worries of residents may be even more intense when they feel alone in the dark. Nights are long if sleep comes only with difficulty. The most troubled require care staff who know them well and move beyond the duties of night watchmen. Unfortunately, one of the most valuable times of the day, the hour or so between bedtime and sleep, coincides with pressures on staff to hurry home and enjoy their leisure. The gap can only be narrowed by active night staff who are sensitive and well briefed.

We know a great deal about sleep, how it occurs and about the distinct movement from drowsiness to real sleep. For some residents it takes a long while to reach deep sleep and, during an eight-hour period, many spend only a short time in such a state. Others may move quickly to deep sleep and remain there until awakened. The benefits of sleep are not necessarily related to the time spent in bed. Some people require much more than others and needs vary with age.

Similar understanding is demanded each morning as staff set about waking large numbers of residents, some eager to busy themselves with the day ahead, others reluctant to leave the security of their beds and a few for whom day or night, sleeping or awake, being up or being in bed, provides no relief from a disturbed and disturbing existence.

With children going to school in the morning, with adults going to work, there must certainly be a sense of urgency created in which an expectation is apparent that they will not be late, and this requires careful thought by staff regarding the time needed to wake residents with forbearance, to respond to those who require individual attention and to allow the opportunity to eat breakfast in a way that is personally satisfying.

If we have a belief in a team concept, then it is at its most important in the morning. It is my experience that staff do not generally allow themselves sufficient time, will regrettably be late on duty, and then pass on their own panic to the residents who live for the next 12 hours with the unfortunate consequences of a rude awakening.

If the residents wish, however, weekends and holidays should be different. Lying in, occasional breakfast in bed, returning to bed after breakfast, or getting up as usual, should all be possible in the same way that these variations are found in people's own homes. There are few worse recipes for tension and aggravation than to find in a residential school all the young people uniformly eating breakfast in a large dining room at 8 am on Sunday morning in preparation for a church service some have no wish to attend.

Food

We turn now to the question of food, the ultimate taste of which stems not only from the intrinsic flavour of what is being eaten, but also from a variety of other conditions. A great deal of symbolism surrounds the preparation and presentation of food. For some people, of seven or 70 years, adapting to new eating patterns on moving from home is not accomplished without discomfort. We must never forget the significance of food in a dependent living situation. Permanent institutional catering can be nauseating to some palates, the absence of certain ingredients in a dish may make food uninviting to many people and the mere preparation by an unfamiliar person – especially if that person represents the system that brought about removal from home – may prevent acceptance and enjoyment of the food being offered. How little we know of the eating habits of the various ethnic and religious groups whose members we find in residential homes; how little we know of their feelings when presented with 'foreign' foods; how little we understand their reasons for picking at meals or rejecting them; and how little we appreciate the internal conflicts through which they must themselves match up the processes of rejection with their needs for survival.

Some time ago I was involved with the unhappy transfer of an adolescent girl from an assessment centre to a children's home. All the changes became marginally tolerable within a few days except for feeding. Forces at work inside Susan did not allow her to eat at the new home. For nearly two months she survived by eating elsewhere and only gradually – in fact at a time of extreme caring when she became ill for a reason seemingly unconnected with her irregular feeding patterns – was she able to accept the nutrition at the home. A clumsy response to Susan's needs could well have led to rejection over a wider span or destructive emotional confrontation. Talking with her both during and after this period gave insight into her inability to take meals in the children's home. Susan had never known her mother and had moved from foster home to foster home, but had promised herself that she would never live in a children's home or, in her own words, become one of the 'forgotten children'. Acceptance of food at the wrong time would have been a personal admission of defeat. She first had to be convinced that a children's home was right for her at that point in her life.

We should talk to residents more about food, bearing in mind that the thought of food will produce a psychic salivary flow which, followed by a tension-free meal, will provide an opportunity for intimacy and conversation. High levels of anxiety drain away the gastric juices and upset the digestive system. I am surprised that in some residential settings staff do not sit at table with residents but only supervise them, often eating their own (better quality) meals later in an adjacent room. As well as adult residents, children and young people should sometimes have the chance to eat out in restaurants in very small groups with members of staff – something in addition to fish and chips hurriedly eaten in semi-darkness in the back of the school minibus – and, in turn, be engaged in the preparation of food for others. Fundamentally, such preparation is a demonstration of what is felt good enough for another person's body. Preparation and the offering of food together with the certainty of choice can say a great deal to the person for whom it is prepared. Feelings about food are intensified in a strange environment. The presentation of new eating patterns to a resident, or giving reassurance about maintaining established dietary habits, requires thought on the part of the care giver.

The attractive presentation of food is to be expected. Awareness of individual preferences and the opportunity to serve oneself at table, and on other occasions to be served, are essential. To a hungry child nothing shows parental love more than an individually prepared plate of egg and chips served by a fond mother. We may rarely be able to approach this level of care (although I ask myself what on earth we are doing when we fail to!), but at least after eating, children, young people and adults should be left, both literally and figuratively, with the right taste in their mouths.

Bodily functions

The feelings surrounding toilet operations may cause humiliation and distress to children, to adolescents, to a number of older residents and to some people with physical handicap. Those who have normally regulated bodily functions are largely unaware of the personal agony resulting from enuresis or encopresis, the embarrassment that can be suffered and the lengths to which an individual has to go in order to conceal problems of wetting and soiling. For some residential staff this is a delicate area for discussion and negotiation, but one which must be spoken about. A peer group label that 'X smells' soon offers a springboard for vigorous emotional reaction in the wake of feelings of being alienated, despised or taunted. There is no straightforward answer in an intimate group environment and the individual can rarely win alone, physiologically, practically or psychologically.

Mandy was an attractive adolescent who moved into residential care at 15 years of age on the death of her foster mother, and soon became ostracized in a girls' hostel because of her incontinence by day and by night. Her personal daytime solution was to stand hour by hour as inconspicuously as possible against the radiator in order to dry her underclothing until one day in response to the increasing gibes of the group her feelings overwhelmed her and she ran away, never to reappear within the remaining three years of her in-care life. Only after her departure were the staff able to think about the pressures to which Mandy had been subjected, about the personal burden which she carried from the hour of admission. Satisfactory as the climate of the hostel appeared, it was not safe enough for Mandy. It was no substitute for the security she had felt in her foster home. Abnormal excretory patterns are difficult to bear given conditions of independence, privacy, choice and complete understanding. The problems are much greater in group living.

For elderly and handicapped people the movement towards increasing dependence on care staff for assistance in going to the toilet or in coping with the problems of wetting or soiling are areas of personal functioning that cause major unhappiness and dejection. Staff have themselves to overcome powerful feelings of nausea and repulsion as they struggle to keep residents clean and dignified. Somehow staff response to this unattractive task in caring for ageing or infirm residents can serve to demonstrate skill, compassion and tolerance which convey to them messages that they are not nuisances, that they are not responsible for weak sphincters, and that they are valued despite the stench that sometimes surrounds them or the mess in which they are frequently found.

Personal possessions
Similarly, we convey a message in the way we show concern for the treasured possessions of a resident. Caring for belongings is another way of caring for the person. The safeguarding of personal possessions can present newcomers to group living with widespread feelings of insecurity. Do residents leave things about as they would at home, and risk having them taken? Do they hand them over to a member of staff, and thereafter have access to them but rarely? Do they carry them around, and thereby chance being regarded as rather strange? Or do they deny the value of personal possessions for themselves and for everybody else and adjudge everything communal?

Any short experience in a residential setting will reveal these four basic patterns, each presenting its peculiar difficulties to individual residents. We must remember that their rights and needs for possessions are no less than those of the care givers. Moving into residential care has probably meant leaving a great deal behind. How does the individual feel about the further loss of a few selected items brought from home? I have been variously entrusted with the faded photograph of a mother who had long since disappeared, with the lock of hair of a deceased daughter, with the one remaining photograph possessed by an adolescent of herself as a baby and with an assortment of animals brought loyally from home at the point of break-up of the family. Each item or creature was at that moment a tangible link with the past in a phase of uncertainty. Staff need to attach the same degree of importance to personal possessions, however seemingly trivial, as does the resident. We all have about us objects which are kept for the feelings surrounding them rather than for their intrinsic value.

The physical environment

A few words about the physical environments we create. Just as we say something by the manner in which we set about the preparation and presentation of food, so the environments we create speak directly to the residents. While some establishments reflect the forethought, ingenuity and artistry of the care givers, others I have visited in the last couple of years have said quite plainly to the residents: 'This is good enough for you'. The most inviting establishments often represent massive efforts to lessen the problems inherent in making pleasing physical provision for groups of people in a semi-public building over which staff and residents have only limited control in matters of decoration, furnishing, equipment or facilities. Society is not willing to spend over-generously on the comfort of those in greatest need, and managers of homes and schools do have difficulties in ordering their priorities when it comes to spending money. But let us make no mistake. We help adults and young people much less effectively if we are unable to demonstrate visually by the environments we build, and in the manner we maintain them, that these are settings worthy of them, settings in which they are valued and cherished.

Smell and noise call for our attention in creating a climate of concern. Some homes and residential schools do smell like institutions. I refer, for example, to the polish we use; to the powerful disinfectants in toilets and bathrooms; to the stench of socks which children continue to wear long after they should have been discarded; and to our failure to eliminate the worst of the cooking smells (and I am not thinking of a roast dinner cooking which can be so inviting to children – and to adults!). If the strong or objectionable nature of these smells is more than we would tolerate in our own homes, what are we doing about them?

At a personal level, there is need for thought to be given to ways of making children, young people and adults more attractive to themselves and to others. For instance, the soap provided in many establishments may be functional and efficient, but does little to encourage its use by the scent it gives off. While showers may have a place in the changing-room of a sports field, a bath gives an opportunity for children, particularly disturbed children, to gratify their whole beings with some of the delightful, and not too expensive, bath cubes, bath salts and bubble baths which, in addition to their soothing properties, help towards building a personally satisfying bodily self-image. There is a natural and instinctive movement, on the part of both adults and other children, towards a sweet-smelling child or young person, perhaps resulting in some form of bodily contact and thus reinforcing his or her appeal as a human being.

Concern for the comfort of residents' bodies is not always apparent. The poor condition of the hair, dirty ears or over-long toenails may go unnoticed for several days while the irritation caused by athlete's foot or severe acne can affect considerably a person's sense of well-being. Careful attention to the treatment of skin complaints, for example, boils, eczema or scabies may prevent a child from feeling wretched about the ugliness of his sores, and lay the foundation for a special relationship. Intimate physical care of the sort often needed in residential homes and schools provides the basis for a different quality of exchange between a resident and a member of staff in other circumstances later in the day.

Noise
A consideration of noise levels is important because our reactions to sound vary, pitch and tone, loudness or softness, harmony or cacophony all bringing about different responses. I know of children who are upset by too much noise and adults who live comfortably amidst a constant din, although we usually associate obliviousness to noise with younger rather than older people. We often pay too little regard to a resident's daily ration of sound (some would say noise). What is the decibel count to which a young child is exposed? What opportunities are there for him to escape

from noise? What provision is made for a resident to be quiet, perhaps in the company of a single member of staff? Carpets in upstairs corridors, bedrooms and lounge areas do more than provide warmth, comfort and a relaxing environment. They also absorb some of the harsh institutional noises.

On the positive side, some stereo sounds offer comfort and bodily relaxation to disturbed, distressed and merely developing young people and adults, reducing anxiety and facilitating communication. We should extend our awareness of this question of sound, for example, by considering the effects of sudden, loud noises. I am thinking especially of adults who find it necessary to shout at young people. We do this for two main reasons: firstly to obtain instant reaction, that is to move somebody, to stop them doing something or to get them to do something; and secondly to assert our control and to demonstrate our authority by expressing anger or displeasure. Adult residents, too, are sometimes shouted at, such behaviour saying in effect: 'I have lost control of you, and of myself, and I must therefore frighten you into submission'.

The fear of staff that 'things will get out of hand' is real and must be one of the greatest discomforts experienced by people in charge of groups of residents, especially adolescents. We may need to look more carefully at what sound is received by a resident rather than what is emitted. Although young people may be unable to avoid listening to unacceptable noises whether addressed to them directly or forming the background to other activities, they may choose rarely to *hear* what is said. I find this distinction between listening and hearing useful both for young people and for adults; indeed, if shouting is perceived as common behaviour in a member of staff, residents will probably 'block off' altogether, thus avoiding as much pain as possible.

Staff–resident communication

Carrying this theme further, I would like more thought to be given to the tone, phrasing and points of emphasis we employ in our verbal exchanges with residents, together with the frequency and the manner in which we use their names. In Chapter 1 reference was made to some of the bizarre practices which surround this question of address. Using a person's given or Christian name thoughtfully is a wonderful way of communicating, of building identity and enhancing self-worth.

We often underestimate the impact of person-to-person contact made by staff members on residents. The hurried gesture of dismissal, the quick movement away and, above all, what we say with our eyes, convey strong messages. With the expressions on our faces we accept or reject, show like or dislike, and say 'come closer' or 'go away'. In answering the demands of residents it is easy to develop what might be described as a 'shop assistant approach' in which the customer is seen as a shadowy figure on the other side of the cash till who receives the standard smile and 'thank you' (if the shop assistant is polite!). On the other hand, it is possible to 'hold' a person, to embrace a resident, with our whole facial expression in a manner that transmits reassuring signals. Do we pay sufficient attention to the visual cues we give young people and adults in our care, both as isolated responses and cumulatively? It is not difficult, in our moments of personal anxiety or distress, for our faces, our whole beings, to register boredom, frustration or dissatisfaction and for these signs to be inappropriately absorbed by residents. If, as I believe, each human interaction is capable of leaving a residue, how great become the responsibilities of residential staff in monitoring the effects of their exchanges with residents. If, after conversation, the residue we leave is one of aggression, anger, disinterest, rejection or alienation, then we merely compound a resident's anxieties, frustrations and difficulties in everyday living.

Education and employment

As part of their overall concern for residents, staff have a responsibility to ensure maximum access to education and employment. The process of admission to a residential setting is disruptive in itself, emotionally, physically and logistically. The time taken up with preliminary visits, tests, medical and psychiatric examinations, court appearances, and the fact that the establishment may temporarily put school or work geographically out of reach of a resident combine to demonstrate that other activities are more important. Where work or school is disliked by a resident, a new set of reasons provides the refuge for further non-attendance.

School and work often represent massive failure zones to residents and, whenever possible, we must reverse these feelings while not conveying our own disappointment in residents when they fail again. A delinquent boy, a disturbed adult or a handicapped person of any age, has no less need to succeed in school or work – however we define success and in whatever setting – than people living in their own homes in the community. It is my belief that many people in residential establishments do not always have equal opportunities in these fields, partly because of the constraints imposed by the settings but more especially by staff caught up in physical care and the emotional conflicts of residents who too readily set aside this primary need for participation in the real world.

It may be unfair to bracket school and work together. Certainly staff seem more inclined to encourage residents to seek employment, but I am worried by the practice of some local authorities whereby children and young people are unnecessarily made to attend school within the residential unit, even for a short while, for no other reason than the convenience of staff, the lack of transport or the pseudo-psychological excuse that there is a need to look at 'the whole child'. Once removed from school in this way, some children never again find their niche. We must keep children in the mainstream of education whenever this is seen to be helping their development or contributing to stability in their lives.

For the child in care, the standard of education we provide within the residential home or school is a cause for concern. I refer readers to a report by members of Her Majesty's Inspectorate called *Community Homes with Education*.[1] While acknowledging the difficulties of teaching in CHEs, giving examples of interesting and purposeful work in some schools, and recognising the commitment of many of the teachers, several areas of disquiet emerge from the survey on which the document is based. Reference is made to the inadequate use made of local education authority support services; the lack of in-service training for teachers; the weak links between CHEs and ordinary schools; the low priority given to careers education; the fragmentation of the curriculum; the absence of curriculum development meetings; the under-development of social education programmes; the *ad hoc* nature of the liaison between teaching and care staff; and the poor systems of classroom record keeping. To these I would add yet another legacy of the past which many schools may still be over-emphasising as part of the basic curriculum, namely, physical education in its broadest sense, and work in trade departments of little relevance in the present economic climate.

These are powerful indictments and, given the same level of criticism in a similar sample of comprehensive schools, there would be parental and public outcries. I noted no reaction to the document from care staff in CHEs, or field staff for that matter, demanding higher standards of educational provision. For boys and girls in residential schools I have a sense that their right to a broad, balanced and stimulating curriculum is of far less political concern. We must make sufficient noise on behalf of 6,500 young people in CHEs and those in residential special schools to ensure that, on compulsory removal from home, educational provision in every way as advantageous as the education provided in their local area is made available to them. Unless we can give some assurance to young people and their parents about this, then we are open to challenge that admission to care for some young people adds a further layer of deprivation: educational deprivation.

We must take to heart the conclusions and recommendations in *Community Homes with Education*, re-examining in each of the 120 schools in England and Wales the potential for satisfying and creative work in the classrooms. I know, and have worked with, many teachers in CHEs throughout the country, and it is time to lift the debate beyond commending them 'for their dedication to the difficult tasks they have undertaken'. Instead, they should be encouraged to develop their teaching expertise in the light of the special needs of children in care, and to establish and expand their professional identity with colleagues and advisors in local education authorities.

I am becoming convinced that, in the long term, social services departments are neither well placed nor equipped to run schools. In 1978 the Warnock Committee[2] recommended that, as a first and major step in improving the quality of educational provision in CHEs, teachers in these establishments should be in the service of local education authorities. The survey by HM Inspectorate adds weight to this argument, perhaps leading to the eventual transfer of the management of CHEs to the education service and to their integration into the range of residential special school provision for children and young people with emotional and behavioural disorders. I would then want to focus attention on the quality of 'care' to be found throughout residential special school provision. In many local education authorities the work has hardly begun, with the mass supervision of large groups of boys or girls by two or three members of staff not uncommon, and infrequent opportunities available for work with individuals or small groups.

The relationship between staff caring for youngsters in children's homes and their teachers in local schools needs consideration. In dealing with the school I would see the role of care staff primarily as that of 'guardian' or 'the concerned adult' and not the professional worker. Children need enthusiastic adults to support their efforts at school, to attend parents' evenings and open days and to communicate with teachers. Naturally, if their own parents can be encouraged to go along to some of these functions so much the better, but this happens all too rarely. There is, I feel, a danger in making the contact an exclusively professional one, working on the 'cases' together, although elements of this are bound to arise from time to time. A label as 'the home children' may destroy a great deal of the work done elsewhere to reduce stigma. Some children, of course, cope with arriving at school in a crowded minibus quite well. Others prefer to alight a few blocks away and to walk the rest of the way like other youngsters.

Concern for the individual

In Chapter 1 some of the handicapping features of residential social work practice were discussed. In this chapter consideration has been given to ways in which it is possible to think positively about the background to the social work task, the care givers' detailed work with residents being less effective where no deliberate attempt is made to develop a climate of concern. In this context, I would like to think about the opportunities provided by the residential establishment, and by the living environments we create, for a person to hold on to his or her uniqueness and to demonstrate individuality, aspects of residential care all too conveniently set aside in our overall responses to the demands of the group.

In an effort to consider each resident as an individual, the practitioner must sometimes cut across the needs of the group. This is undoubtedly one of the tensions inherent in the work, where a fine balance must constantly be kept between the needs of the group and the needs of the individual. In residential social work the group process is often under-valued as a primary means of helping the individual and our skills remain under-developed in this respect. Nevertheless, the ultimate goal is the strengthening of the individual. The group has no intrinsic value other than as a vehicle for its members, and an objective eye must be kept on the power of the group as it seeks to submerge the needs of one or two of its members, either by its organisational structures or the therapeutic process.

Several people have a role to play in keeping alive the importance of the individual: the care staff in the home or school; the key worker, if one exists; the external manager; any independent visitor; and members of a resident's family. The extent to which such monitoring is possible will say a great deal about the establishment as a whole, and about the attitudes of its internal managers.

Many residents will not allow themselves to be submerged, asserting themselves on every possible occasion. They have a right to do so. Their mental health is probably assured more than that of residents who slide into the routine without question and accept the regulations with unnatural compliance.

Any analysis by a resident of a 24-hour period may give cause for self-assertion: being awakened brusquely; being settled too hurriedly at night; being called to another activity halfway through a favourite television programme; receiving abuse from fellow residents; having less than a fair share of food or attention; experiencing anger because a fieldworker has not arrived as arranged; or even being let down by the staff at the home. All these appear valid reasons for forceful self-expression on the part of a resident.

Staff may not like a resident's way of showing displeasure. They may be unhappy about the organisational structure or the group pressures preventing the resident from being shown greater consideration, but feel helpless to change things. Their task, however, is 'to hear the resident out' and, as far as possible, to place themselves in that position, displaying understanding of the issue that caused the resident to put forward a strong opinion. From the resident's point of view, the comments are frequently not without some substance.

Where there is no immediate resolution or worthwhile compromise, and residents are seen to be adversely affected by internal arrangements or administratively-oriented external management, the staff are bound to defend the rights of residents by taking up their worries through all legitimate channels and finding new ones as necessary. Those who are working closely with a group of people should be the first to recognise when rights are being ignored and take action accordingly. We cannot rule out involvement in political action on major issues. Who else speaks for residents? Who has greater knowledge of the intimacies of their lives?

A complaints procedure should be established in every home, one which is uncomplicated, visible, swift in resolution and trusted by the residents. Without such a safety valve, staff power, in some instances, becomes absolute. Our knowledge of the consequences of concentrated power should be sufficient to convince staff of the dangerous possibilities for omnipotence in residential homes and schools.

Suggestion boxes, residents' committees and community meetings have their place in furthering the work of establishments, while complaints procedures are aimed particularly at individual grievances that residents are unable to resolve for themselves by the

SECTION F

The Social Services Committee is a group of men and women who have been voted on to the County Council by the people in Durham and have to look after the Social Services in County Durham. Mr. Trietline, the Director of Social Services has thought a lot about how children in care should and should not be treated and he made up a list of what he thought would be ill-treatment if it happened. He asked the *Committee* what they thought and they agreed with him.

What comes next tells you what ill-treatment is, and what to do about it if you think *you* are being ill-treated.

What is 'Ill-Treatment'

It is:—

(1) *All* forms of punishment to the body, for example striking, slapping, smacking, shaking or kicking.

(2) Not letting you have your meals.

(3) Stopping you visiting your parents when it has already been agreed.

(4) Actions by staff, that make you look small, such as not talking to you; being blamed for everything; being made to wear second-hand clothes or clothes that don't fit you; or being kept in pyjamas all day or being made a fool of, etc.

(5) Being locked up in a room.

(6) When the staff run down your parents to you or other children.

(7) Being punished when you wet your pants or your bed.

(8) Anything that takes away your dignity or self-respect, in other words, makes you feel small.

But Remember—The staff have to have some control or the place would be a shambles and not fit to live in. This is what they *can* do if you don't behave yourself:

(1) Stop you going on outings or playing out; stop you watching T.V.

(2) Give you extra work to do in the Home.

(3) Hold your pocket money back.

(4) Make you pay for any damage you cause, from part of your pocket money.

(5) Take any dangerous things (such as knives and matches, etc.) away from you.

(6) Stop you hurting other children.

(7) Defend themselves, if you attack them.

(8) Stop you damaging things.

Sometimes the person doing the ill-treating doesn't realise he is doing it. Sometimes adults do things to children "for their own good" and what they do can amount to ill-treatment. The Social Services hope that this never happens in Durham. But it might, and this is why the next bit has been put in this book.

'Ill Treatment and What to Do'

If you feel you are being ill-treated by *anyone*, either inside or outside the place where you are living, then you should do something about it.

You should do this by telling the head of your establishment or your social worker, who will do their best to sort things out.

If you are not satisfied with what is done, you should post the "Contact Card" which is in the pocket at the back of this booklet.

All you have to do is to write your name on the card and put it in a letter box. You don't need to put a stamp on it. The card is addressed to Mr. P. C. Trietline, the Director of Social Services at County Hall, Durham, who will send someone to see you.

If you think a young child is being ill-treated in your Home and the child is too young to post a *"Contact Card"* then you should do it for him or her.

Section F, *Guide for Children in Care* (Durham County Council, 1979) usual means. People living in a residential home or school will occasionally feel crushed by the decisions of others, for example, in transferring them to an establishment many miles away, limiting contact with a friend or relative or setting boundaries on their life-styles that they find intolerable. We cannot rule out the need to complain to an independent person about harsh sanctions or physical punishment. Learning to use a complaints procedure responsibly and without malice or fear is part of the wider educational process in which staff should be engaged. It is essential for later healthy survival in the community.

Some local authorities have given a lead in upholding rights and investigating complaints, especially in child care practice. Durham County Council's booklet, *Guide for Children in Care*, is a model of its kind (see Section F, reproduced here) and the handbook produced by the London Borough of Camden for young people in care, *Straight Answers*, is packed with information for the resident in difficulty. Both include pre-paid cards addressed to the Director of Social Services. Several other local authorities are in the process of tailoring schemes to the work of their agencies. This is one of the most exciting developments of recent years, and we are moving into an era of 'due process' previously unknown in residential settings. I also hope that the idea spreads more in homes for adults, perhaps linked to the prospectuses discussed earlier.

Staff will usually acknowledge the merits of a complaints procedure to the extent that they accept the resident's right to be different.[3] We are destined to be different from the moment of conception. The circumstances under which we were conceived, how we were nurtured during the nine months before birth, and every detailed interaction that takes place thereafter between us and our environments, determine how we are at any given moment. We are all delightfully different by virtue of our genetic composition and our environmental upbringing. For this reason we can never move completely into other people's worlds, they can never be like us, and we can never make them like us. Indeed we should question our right to do so. Kahlil Gibran takes up this point:

Your children are not your children.
. . . though they are with you yet they belong not to you.
You may give them your love but not your thoughts,
For they have their own thoughts.
You may house their bodies but not their souls,
For their souls dwell in the house of tomorrow, which you cannot visit, not even in your dreams.

You may strive to be like them, but seek not to make them like
   you.
For life goes not backward nor tarries with yesterday.
You are the bows from which your children as living arrows are
   sent forth.[4]

Our society, our institutions, our schools have a tendency to want
to make people the same. Sometimes we become fixated on
developmental milestones, on age-related behaviour, on age-appropriate activities and on what we think is best for another person. I
would defend the individual's right to be different. George Bernard
Shaw had an enigmatic thought on the subject:

> The reasonable man adapts himself to the world: the unreason-
> able one persists in trying to adapt the world to himself. There-
> fore all progress depends on the unreasonable man.[5]

There is for each person a point between our duties and our responsibilities where he or she has the optimum chance of asserting
the right to be different. We are bound to help the individual find
that point. By virtue of our employment contract with local
authorities we have a duty to protect society and its members from
the damaging aspects of idiosyncratic behaviour. As residential
social workers we have a responsibility to those in our care to allow
them maximum free expression of their personalities and the
opportunity to indulge individual needs and whims. As employees
we have a duty to receive into our specialised establishments those
who have become enmeshed in self-damaging conflicts in their
families, their schools and their local communities; as professionals
we have a responsibility to ensure that nothing we do in our residential homes and schools perpetuates these struggles against often
unidentified enemies.

For each admission to a residential setting we are confronted
with two people: the person as he or she is and the person society
would like him or her to be.[6] In trying to satisfy the demands of
society, we must not reject the real person, because deep within him
or her is an individual story to tell and an individual life to enact.
As John Holt reminds us:

> What we need to realize ... is that our power over another
> person's life is at most very limited and that if we try to extend
> that power beyond that narrow limit we do so only by taking
> from him his ability to control his own life. The only way we can
> fully protect someone against his own mistakes and the
> uncertainties of the world is to make him a slave. He is then

defenceless before *our* whims and weaknesses. Most people would prefer to take their chances with the world. They have a right to that choice.[7]

3 The Social Work Task

Discussions continue about residential social work as part of social work or as a discrete activity requiring specific skills. Generic training has undoubtedly contributed to the loss of a great deal of earlier accumulated wisdom about responses to the particular needs of various client groups in residential settings. Gradually, however, we are again establishing a more solid foundation for the practice of residential social work. The publication of guidelines by local authority social services departments, the formulation of aims and objectives for every home and the development of care plans for each individual resident provide a background for the task which, in my opinion, remains a firm part of social work practice while requiring additional knowledge and special abilities on the part of the worker in matters of self-management, tenacity and emotional resilience.

A central feature of residential social work practice is this question of self-management in the face of constant exposure to residents, often competing in each other's presence for a worker's time, attention and emotional investment. The place of supervision and consultancy as a partial response to this will be taken up later.

A closer definition of social work in residential settings and the capacity to put it into practice mean a better deal for residents, while increasing for the workers both the demands on them as vital human resources and the corresponding rewards and satisfactions which controlled immersion in the lives of residents inevitably brings.

The following list of social work tasks is by no means exhaustive. Some settings will require further refinement of the definitions. Others will find some headings irrelevant to their work. If, however, in the case of those acknowledged as essential, we keep them to the front of our minds in drawing up policy, in managing the group, in making decisions and in working with individual residents, then there is greater likelihood that the people we are working with will not only survive but thrive. And that may be the major difference between caring for people and working with them. It is the task of residential social workers to:

★ encourage age-related independence;
★ foster appropriate dependence;
★ promote interdependence;

★ offer understanding of the complexities of living in a group;
★ work purposefully and in depth on the problem areas that brought about admission to residential care;
★ identify good experiences in the earlier life of a resident and build on these;
★ compensate for the lack of good early experiences;
★ lessen intrapersonal conflicts, or help someone cope with them;
★ work with residents in reducing the level of their impulsive behaviour;
★ respond with tolerance to the day-to-day crises presented by the individuals or groups within the home or school;
★ demonstrate an understanding of behaviour and the underlying causes of anxiety and distress;

★ provide a backcloth for normal development;
★ keep alive the concept of normality;

★ provide opportunities for the development of social skills;
★ develop trust and the ability to be trusted, for example with money, by being truthful and honest, and in the management of time;
★ help residents use money with forethought;
★ create for residents opportunities for the demonstration of responsible behaviour;

★ enable residents to enjoy the present;
★ make the residential setting a base for other activities;
★ facilitate the growth of personal relationships;
★ acknowledge the residents as sexual beings;

★ present, in the case of young people, the best possible models of adulthood;

★ help residents prepare for the future.

These may be high-sounding phrases, and they will certainly only be as valuable as our ability to translate them into action. Human conduct, human emotions and the rights of man are all embraced by care givers as they work with residents on these basic initiatives and responses. They may not succeed as often as they would wish. They may not succeed if others deny the importance of the corner stones I am putting in place. Without the intellectual, emotional and practical support of managers, administrators and members, practitioners become vulnerable.

It is pertinent to ask: Are these all social work tasks? In isolation, some definitions may be challenged. After all, it does not require training and expertise to help somebody 'enjoy the present', 'use money with forethought' or 'present a model of adulthood'. In many instances the detail of the tasks can only be successfully addressed with the co-operation and involvement of people in the community far removed from social work practice. Part of the residential social workers' responsibilities must, therefore, lie in ascertaining need, facilitating opportunities, monitoring responses, and providing the checks and balances essential for the progress of residents within the broad band of human growth, development and aspiration. Sometimes all the tasks discussed in this chapter will necessarily be undertaken for a short while by residential social workers, especially with the most distressed and handicapped residents soon after admission. Later, many will be shared, worked on with the individual resident, and ideally handed over completely as people prepare for independent living, make relationships of their own choosing or demonstrate sufficient strength to manage their own affairs. Consequently, a further task may be to return to residents with the utmost speed control of those areas of their lives which were snatched away on moving from home.

Acceptance of the tasks suggested in this chapter will increase stress in the worker. The tasks require both involvement and distancing; giving direct assistance and helping others to help themselves; and, above all, being sensitive to the present needs of the individual residents. Giving to others in a way which aids their development is tiring, demanding and sometimes irksome. Giving in a way which allows them to realign and even to reshape whole areas of their lives calls for skill and understanding naturally available to very few people; and for sacrifices usually reserved for those within our most intimate personal networks. Occasionally residents may become part of these networks. Only when these two strands of personal giving are visible does it become legitimate to describe residential social work as 'professional'.

Independence

By its very nature residential living militates against the encouragement of independent thought and action. First, there is comparatively such a wealth of primary provision in terms of food, warmth, laundry, furnishings, companionship, entertainment and organisation that pervasive forces are at work which not only dissuade but actively prevent individuals from exercising the everyday decisions common to us all. They rarely have to think about the milkman, the plumber or the state of the kitchen; in some establishments, even what to eat, what to wear or when to take a bath are decisions made by others. Secondly, a person's presence in a residential setting may mean that earlier freedom of independent action has led to trouble with the law or caused intolerable conflict within the family or local community. Thirdly, there is an inbuilt reluctance on the part of residential social workers to encourage aspects of independence in which residents have the possibility of failure. On the one hand this may be for the good reason that they see it as potentially damaging to the individual to fail again or to run the risk of being caught stealing. On the other hand, I suspect that they feel more intensely that it is the care givers who must often bear the consequences of residents' unsound judgements and therefore limit their independence to areas of personal behaviour where the outcome is unimportant.

It takes only a little while for a resident to lose the will to think and act independently, and for staff to regard as disruptive a person who will not allow this to happen. With adults we may not even notice the process taking place. With children and young people we easily lose sight of the numerous opportunities for controlling their own lives that most youngsters at home enjoy today: in spending their money, in their style of dress, in rearranging their bedroom furniture, in choosing their friends and in leisure time activities. The problem lies not only in our measurement of what we think is age-related independence for residents, and particularly adolescents, but in what they feel is their due as they make comparisons with the lifestyles of their mates. For young people in residential care the gap between what would seem to them age-appropriate independence and what they are allowed to do in practice may be unnaturally widened by the nature of group living and by the care givers' knowledge of how residents handled independence before coming into care, the latter sometimes making staff over-cautious.

Risk taking, which must anticipate failure as well as success, is inherent in encouraging independence. The testing ground includes the criteria used by staff to determine the right level of independence for any particular individual, and the manner in which we react when mishaps occur.

Dependence

There is a place within the residential setting for dependent relationships. Healthy independence can only grow out of earlier opportunities for a non-handicapping dependent relationship, an experience unfamiliar to some people prior to admission. Sometimes, of course, residents will have enjoyed first-class dependent relationships that can be transferred and developed on their road to maturity. On other occasions, however, residents will have been so badly let down that they cannot bear to become dependent again; or have grown up with extreme deprivation; or have been suffocated by others whose own needs to have another person dependent upon them have been pre-eminent. Mentally handicapped people, physically handicapped people, elderly people and children of all ages may have been affected in this way. The residual feelings remaining from an earlier, warm, dependent relationship and from intermittent temporary dependency later in life are integral parts of most of our developmental experiences, sometimes unknown to residents.

Enabling the right levels of dependency to exist, and using these to promote the later independence of residents is a key aspect of residential work. This is especially important where staff are working towards later independent living for those in their care, for example a young person eventually going out of care or a physically handicapped person moving to his or her own accommodation.

Some residents will, for the wrong reasons, never allow themselves to become dependent. Others will swiftly be drawn into heavily dependent relationships either with individual members of staff or with the establishment as a whole. Both are potentially destructive to the individual. In cases of reduced mobility, loss of bodily control or illness, whether permanent or temporary, residents may need encouragement to become dependent, a difficult adjustment after perhaps 50 or more years of independent living. Staff, too, may find it difficult to achieve the right balance with elderly or handicapped people. Mostly our satisfactions are obtained from working with people who progress. Progress for increasingly handicapped people may have to be measured by their ability to accept with dignity their right to become dependent.

Interdependence

I see as highly desirable the ability of human beings to become interdependent, a goal no less for residents than for ourselves. Such a state may be experienced in friendship, in crisis or in marriage which, at their best, provide models for reciprocity in relationships. Staff and residents are at a disadvantage in homes and schools because organisational structures and role requirements work against the growth of interdependent relationships. They do, however, occur from time to time. Young people and adults on camping expeditions experience role blurring in many instances as do residents and staff in a crisis, for example in making a joint protest against the outside world when a decision is being made to close a home or school, or in responding to an unforeseen staff shortage. Often staff will say that such occasions 'bring out the best in residents'. Remarks like this have implications for our work, for the way we organise residential care, and for the seriousness with which we provide opportunities for the growth of such relationships. Most residential care works against the concept of interdependence between staff and residents, between residents and their friends in the community, and even between the residents themselves.

It is a unique experience to move with a resident from a position as 'subordinate object' – and, if we are honest, we know that many residents always remain in this state, however we attempt to disguise the fact – to that of a completely accepted person where role differences no longer exist.

I can recall a number of residents with whom I eventually sensed a feeling of mutuality, residents admitted with the most serious problems and by no means overcome when we became aware of a different quality in the relationship. The residents' status was no longer a threat to me; my power base no longer concerned them; it began to feel wrong for a dozen people, several of whom had never met the residents concerned, to sit around a table to discuss them as cases; their problems remained worrying but did not overwhelm me; and, most profitably, I was able to engage in open communication of a quality not universally found in resident–staff contacts. Conversation took place on a different level, intellectually and emotionally. What I also experienced, and I am thinking particularly of three very angry residents, was the disappearance from their lives of the verbal and physical violence that had for so many years formed the basis of their exchanges with other people. In one instance the power base was immediately tipped after a 16-year old boy helped me to control another resident who had gone berserk, was systematically smashing the windows and about to push a fistful of broken glass into my face.

The complexities of group living

I turn now to the need to offer newcomers an understanding of the complexities of living in a group. In a residential home most aspects of life are made visible – to other residents, to care staff and to domestic staff. Contact may also be made, either voluntarily or as part of the culture, with a range of visiting experts. In the first instance, and often for a long time, the resident will have little idea of the roles many of these people are fulfilling. They may be permanent or temporary members of staff, experienced or inexperienced, students or agency employees, powerful or powerless, and appear to change every few hours. In a very short space of time many different people will be giving orders, asking questions, making demands, having expectations, requesting explanations, suggesting alternatives, demonstrating concern and encouraging participation, all in the name of kindness, control, 'treatment' and good practice.

For a person who has had a very private life the constant exposure to others is extremely taxing for both mind and body. It is difficult for the resident to make sense of the group process of which he or she becomes an integral part from the moment of stepping through the door. The individual will feel warmth, or anger, or rejection, or fear for no other reason than that of being there, there to receive whatever members of the group care to offer or deny, often the immediate reflection of what they themselves are experiencing. Little wonder it often takes time to settle down.

Prior to the reception of a new member into the group, work must be undertaken with both the existing members, residents and staff, and with the new person. There is a natural resistance by staff to welcoming somebody who has a potential for disruption and residents do not always give up unselfishly their share of the space, affection and attention received by staff.

At first a resident may not be able to present his or her best side, or most endearing qualities, due to feeling angry, depressed, withdrawn or violent; or to the need to put on a brave face or to present a tough image. Reminding other residents of their own emotions on moving away from home or transferring from another establishment, and working with the associated feelings, may be helpful and I have sometimes been aware of residents displaying the most responsible behaviour towards a new member of the group when they have been enabled to participate fully in the process. Only disaster can result from a precipitate admission where neither residents nor staff have advance warning – something that still occurs all too frequently.

Working on residents' problems
The decision to admit a client to a residential setting may be made

by unknown people. Often the individual concerned will not be in agreement and may even be extremely hostile to the idea. This being the case, it behoves us to work purposefully and in depth for as long as necessary on the problem areas that brought about admission. I sense here a moral obligation to be active in the task, for the agency through its practitioners to be held accountable in planning, tackling and monitoring their attack on problem areas in the residents' lives. For society to intervene with the force of law and authority, and then to respond merely with *physical* care should cause greater discomfort to practitioners, administrators and politicians than it seemingly does. Comparatively few establishments address this issue in the necessary depth. There is a general feeling that staff too often *live* with residents rather than *work* with them.

The residential social worker has two principal approaches in working with residents: (1) through the experience of daily living; and (2) through the special times set aside for individual and group-work. I am not convinced that we place sufficient value on daily living as a vehicle for change and stress reduction, although traditionally this has been one of the first 'lessons' taught to residential social workers in training. It has been suggested that staff are less aware than they were 20 years ago of the uses to be made of getting up, mealtimes and going to bed – occasions for conversation and demonstrations of concern which are referred to in some detail in the previous chapter.

Tackling personal difficulties at an individual or group level throughout a person's stay in a residential home or school is work from which some staff withdraw. It must, however, be one of our next moves forward, building into all care programmes the opportunity for small group meetings to discuss aspects of growing up; the problems of leaving home; and what it means to be 'in care'. Some staff will be able to use a group to work on the problems of the individual: why Mary cannot face staying at home for more than two hours at a time; how John can be helped to be less noisy and disruptive at mealtimes; or how to assist Sara to find a means of expressing her anger and frustration other than by putting her fist through a window, slashing her wrist or refusing to eat. Equally, most people in residential care may also have personal worries that are best talked about on a one-to-one basis. And I am not here referring to crisis interventions, mediating and placating which fill the on-duty hours of so many staff.

Individuals can contain anxieties if they are certain of a regular·

time of their own for discussion about what concerns them most. Many staff feel apprehensive about working closely with residents, particularly adolescents, whose social histories show problems of a sexual nature or those relating to violence or depression. Some will argue for an outsider with specialist skill. I have no doubt, however, that the work involved in tackling these personal problems can be competently handled by trained residential staff, and I am concerned that a person, perhaps removed from home against his or her will, can spend a number of years in a school or home and never have continuing discussions with a trusted member of staff which give some hope of working through the feelings surrounding earlier disquieting events. I am reminded of a boy I had contact with in a CHE. Removed from home at 14 years of age following an incident in which he had interfered with two young girls, he settled quickly in the school and was thought ready to return home after less than a year. As a date approached for him to leave I could not identify one single occasion on which he had had the opportunity to talk freely to a single adult about the act leading to his court appearance. For whatever reasons, those caring for him had failed in their primary task.

Identifying good experiences
A starting point is the need for the identification of good experiences in the resident's earlier life. It is on these that we build. The extent to which it is possible to reinforce good experiences will determine the eventual direction of a resident. Bombarded by negative information at the time of admission we may neglect strengths, actual and potential, because there is a tendency to view residents as more inadequate, more devious and less able to manage parts of their lives than is frequently the case. We must remember that for several years an adult may have been living in the community: using public transport, making telephone calls, shopping, going to bingo, the cinema, the theatre, the post office or the pub, and mixing with a variety of people. However small, a bank of good experience will have been built up through previous associations, achievements and relationships. People will have been attracted to the individual, who will have given to other people in the way that giving is its own reward, perhaps very different from the way the new care givers understand. He or she will remember help received; will have demonstrated loyalty; infant years may have been well spent; the person may have loved and been loved; may feel passionately about animals, the countryside, boxing, cooking or snooker, all of

which give hope for the future. Too quickly these earlier good experiences, associations and feelings may be lost on taking up residence.

Compensating for damaging experiences

Only after the identification of good experiences will we be able to develop strategies to compensate for earlier unhelpful experiences. These developmental disabilities may occur over the whole range of educational, social and emotional experience and need to be talked about formally as soon as possible by those most intimately concerned with the resident's future. In some establishments a preliminary case conference is held for this purpose about a month after a person comes to live in the home. This is an effective way of proceeding, used as it can be to stress the urgency for action and to allocate the particular responsibilities of field, residential and managerial staff during the coming months. With another conference five months later, and intensive work in between, in most instances it should become clear during this time whether rehabilitation, a modified lifestyle, an alternative lifestyle or a further period of residential care is indicated. This early concentrated effort probably offers the opportunity for our most important work with residents.

Intrapersonal conflict

Working in detail on the problem areas that brought about admission to residential care is often inseparable from the need to lessen intrapersonal conflicts, or help someone to cope with them. My earlier examples (pp. 17–19) from the lives of Carol, Mrs Ashton, Malcolm, Kevin and Meg Johnson illustrate how, almost invariably, movement away from all that is familiar is likely to produce stress within the individual. A child may feel guilty about engineering her own departure from a family, or she may fear rejection; an adult may regret his violent behaviour, his inability to hold down a job or his excessive drinking. Until the weight of these feelings has been shared and explored they may manifest themselves as anger, withdrawal or denial, all potential barriers to the restoration of an individual to life in the community.

Tina was 18 years of age when she went into a residential home. She had been physically handicapped since birth, attributable, she believed, to the violence that occurred between her parents when her mother was pregnant. On taking up residence, Tina had little will to live. She tells her own story:

I was thirteen when dad called me into the kitchen. He was sitting on the table. My mother was standing in front of the fridge.

'Tina', he said, 'Your mother and I are going to split up. We find that our marriage hasn't been working out lately, so we've decided to separate. It seems right to tell you before you go back to boarding school'.

There was nothing to say. It was just put into words what I had been holding in my heart. Just before Christmas my mother had had a cold and 'so that daddy wouldn't catch it' she had moved into the spare room. There were never any quarrels but, gradually, I realised that it was more than a cold because she never went back to the other bedroom.

When I went home for the summer holidays, dad had left. Mother had taken a lodger, introduced to me as Steve, and he had a room above the garage. 'Please, Tina', mother said, 'don't go near Steve's room. He likes to be quiet and we don't want to disturb him'.

Always obedient, I did as I was told. Strange, though, mother's bedclothes were never ruffled, even first thing in the morning. It was a shock to accept that she was sleeping with Steve. From that moment my loneliness was complete. Father had gone away and visited me once a term at school. Mother had given herself to Steve and was embarrassed by my presence in the house. Holidays were tense. I had never liked Steve and told her so, frequently and with conviction, but not in his presence. Tears held back in term time flowed freely in the quiet of my bedroom.

'Of course, my dear,' mother would say, 'I'd never marry Steve unless you were in agreement'. Before I had returned home again, however, she had done just that, and Steve was my step-father. Uncle Frank, mother's brother, came to school to tell me the news, bringing a note from my mother, also signed by Steve.

Shortly afterwards we moved. I learned a little more about Steve. He had held several important jobs in building, but his excessive drinking habits had forced him to resign each one. By the time I was 17 and on the point of leaving school, he was an alcoholic, unable to work, a chain-smoker and a gambler who squeezed all the money he could out of my mother. I was a cripple forced to share the same house.

Mother was the bread-winner, letting out two rooms in the house to foreign students, mostly girls about 18 years of age, who were taking short courses at the English Language Study Centre a mile down the road. She prepared some meals and was supposed to offer the atmosphere of an English family household together with conversation practice. I suddenly became useful, providing English conversation and friendship, even having to give up my room on occasion so that an extra 'paying guest' could be accommodated. How I came to hate these visitors; to hate 'him'; and to despise my mother for the burden she had so foolishly taken on. In my last term of school mother had a nervous breakdown, and was in hospital for several weeks.

'I have to take it easy with drink now,' she said, 'It wouldn't take much for me to slip like Steve.'

The lengthy struggle to overcome some of Tina's handicaps, physical and emotional, is not yet over. She will always be different, but the effects of 13 years in a residential school have been talked about, the strengths and weaknesses of her experiences identified, her intelligence appreciated, licence to make friends where she will has been given and she now has a job in a travel agency.

There is a will to live, and a will to live to the full. I have been unable to pinpoint all the factors contributing to Tina's success, but I can suggest five: a climate within the residential home in which normality rather than pathology is stressed; a freedom of movement and action inside and outside the home; a spacious room of her own; an atmosphere in which the past and the present can be safely discussed both individually and in groups; and a male member of staff who works with Tina and who sees Tina rather than her handicap. Overall, intrapersonal conflicts have been reduced, and Tina has been given the means to cope with those that remain.

Impulsive behaviour

Many residents need to lessen the frequency of their impulsive behaviour. Such behaviour may take many forms, including violent outbursts when their will is opposed, shoplifting, running away and self-injury. It is the unpredictable nature of their responses that staff find so infuriating, but unless greater self-controls are acquired by the individual the stay in a residential home may be prolonged. A well established pattern of behaviour is not easily reversed, although often such impulsive reactions may be connected with more recent events. This distinction needs to be made. Because of the specific nature of the task, a considerable degree of success is possible with residents in respect of their impulsive behaviour. First, it is important to link unacceptable behavioural responses to the events that apparently trigger them off, and to engage the residents in improving their own self-control. They will require help with this. As is the case when dealing with young children, staff need to anticipate well by planning residents' time and the pattern of their activities in a manner that offers less likelihood for impulsive reaction, to acknowledge with the residents those occasions when frustration does not lead to problematic responses and for these to be rewarded by discussion and encouragement. Praise must be generous for limited progress. It is on this that we build. For an adolescent girl who always opens up a wound on her arm following a weekly visit from her father, there are numerous diversions possible as a less painful alternative, but staff have to be creative and patient. For a boy who runs away when challenged by an authority figure, progress may mean still running away, but not so far. I have often suggested to a young, disturbed boy that he *should* run and hide in the garden or in another room or even in the local park instead of running all the way home. It has often brought about the desired result by becoming a game and later having no meaning at all.

Responding to crisis

Staff reaction to impulsive behaviour is, of course, part of their task in responding with tolerance to the day-to-day crises presented by the individuals or groups within the home or school. Residents do not always find tolerance in their care givers as they struggle with their individual or group problems. For many people their very presence in a residential unit means that they have suffered personal difficulties. The new and initially unnatural experience of group living is bound to produce tensions among those finding their place in the home. Threats, blame and sanctions will only worsen already delicate relationships. Residents will push staff to respond in a manner experienced in earlier parts of their lives, and we often fall into their traps unconsciously, reinforcing expectations and alienation. Every unhappy incident with a resident, every unfortunate occurrence within a group can be used by staff and worked with as a vehicle for learning.

It is the staff member, however, who has to accept responsibility for initiating the learning from each event. Tolerance on its own makes for insecurity within individuals and within the group because they feel without boundaries. The emergence, definition and redefinition of boundaries occurs in the non-punitive response of staff intent on using day-to-day events, important or unimportant, within the individual or within the group, as a model for handling other incidents away from the residential setting.

It is sometimes the intolerance of residents that has brought about their admission to residential care – with their companions in school, with members of their family, with their husbands or wives. There is little merit in staff replicating residents' intolerant behaviour. There is merit in providing residents with tools for healthy survival in their lives outside the home or school.

Understanding behaviour

This aspect of staff response is carried further in their frequent demonstrations of understanding of behaviour and the underlying causes of anxiety and distress. Now we are at the heart of residential social work. Anxiety and distress pervade the residential scene in a concentrated form unknown elsewhere. Easing emotional pain, lessening anxiety and alleviating distress are the prerequisites of a return to 'normal' functioning and while the activities are concurrent rather than sequential, this very human aspect of our work demands a corresponding emotional investment from the care givers.

Violence, withdrawal, crying and anger are all observable incidents of behaviour stemming from deeply-rooted and deeply-felt traumata which individuals have been carrying for a short or a long while and which have now erupted. In working with people in residential settings, whether for assessment purposes or in long-term care, more time and thought should be given to relating the expression of residents' often overwhelming personal experiences – so hastily punished, misinterpreted or used as a reason for rejection – to their internal states. Certainly we go some way towards this in our daily approaches to care. I do not think that we go far enough. The following account of an episode of violence illustrates for me the importance of relating behaviour to the heavy emotional burdens carried by many residents:

Alan, aged ten, had been living at the assessment centre for five weeks. He had been to court twice: on 2 February and on 23 February. On the first occasion he was made the subject of an interim order and three weeks later a care order was made. Some of the other boys said that he had 'got eight years' but he did not understand. He *did* know that it was 'his' conference at the beginning of April and that today, Monday 8 March, he was in bed and it only seemed like four o'clock in the afternoon.

Alan had been home for the weekend, the first time since coming into care, and he had returned to the centre on Sunday evening. Throughout Saturday and Sunday he had overheard terrible outbursts of anger between his parents, especially on Saturday evening, during which his father had threatened once again to leave his mother and the three other children. His mother had spoken softly, and he had only heard the murmur of her voice going on and on.

In the rush of coming back on Sunday evening and settling down, there has not been a suitable moment for Alan to speak about his anxiety to a 'special' grown-up. The adult to whom he would have wished to communicate his worries as he had done in the past was on leave anyway. This worker was kind and gentle: she always listened intently, was appalled by his father's outbursts and deeply sorry for his mother. It comforted Alan to talk to her. When Alan's mother had called at the assessment centre, Mary, this worker, had listened to her complaints about her husband ... Alan's father had never visited.

On Monday morning Alan did not seem too worried, but was chatting to the other children and to the care staff as the boys were dressing. One of them said, 'I wonder whether it's going to rain ...' and Alan replied, 'Of course not, look how blue the sky is' (there were quite a few dark clouds). He was not hungry at breakfast. He did not remember much about going into the classroom and starting work. Later his teacher, who was a man Alan liked well, asked him to write a composition about 'My Weekend'. Suddenly the whole horror of the situation at home came back to his mind: he sat, staring in front of him, and was startled when the teacher asked him 'What's wrong?'. Alan started to write 'I went to the cinema ...'. At lunchtime he was still not hungry. He felt very full, as though something was choking him. People asked him if he was ill, but he shook his head. Anything said to him now seemed like a blow, which made him wince, and any contact became intolerable. He no longer knew what was causing him so much anguish. He did not know what seemed to engulf him. He went out after lunch into the playground in a daze.

Suddenly another boy punched him in the back. This was not a hard punch, but Alan felt a burning behind his nose, he shivered all over and turned white. In an instant, he had thrown himself screaming on the other boy, knocked him down and tried to strangle him. Staff intervened, and with difficulty pulled Alan away from the boy he was attacking and held him while he screamed and kicked. They tried to understand what had gone wrong, but he was too distressed to speak or even think. He was put to bed for the rest of the day.

On the following morning he got up as usual ...[1]

Encouraging normality

Questions about the provision of a backcloth for normal development and the need to keep alive the concept of normality are important in residential work. If we so choose it is possible to identify pathology all around us to the exclusion of the immense areas of normality displayed by residents. It is often only a tiny part of their lives that has been defined as unacceptable, too disconcerting for their families to handle or too embarrassing for their communities to cope with. With any person experiencing a problem, the solution is frequently to be found in our ability to build on normality, a process that inevitably eases inner conflict or lessens anti-social behaviour.

Unfortunately many residential establishments feed into the abnormality, pain, distress and delinquency of the residents by their structures, their routines, their suspicion, their restrictions, their pettiness, their excessive controls, their authoritarian or patronising attitudes and their inability to return to first principles, to identify what is needed for residents to merge with people in the surrounding community and to promote patterns of living based on these concepts.

It takes very little for residents to become markedly different from everybody else at work, at school or at play. We scarcely know it is happening, and many residential staff redefine normality because they themselves have moved into an artificial world. Unless we develop hyper-sensitivity to this, and are constantly challenged about daily practice, ourselves making a frequent analysis of our attitudes, instructions and expectations when working with residents, then as likely as not we are merely contributing to their abnormality.

In Chapter 1 I listed some of the horrific practices still found in residential homes and schools in this country, many of which point to the abnormality of staff rather than residents. The notion of stigma has been around for a long while. Intellectually it is an attractive and uncomplicated concept to absorb and to wrestle with. In practice it spreads through our work like a cancer, from the simple act of making a child bring a receipt for the 15p he has paid for his school swimming ticket so that the local authority can check that the money really has been spent to the anger and frustration of the physically handicapped adult unable to entertain a member of the opposite sex freely in his or her room.

There is a small pub in London near a hostel for very quiet, friendly, mentally handicapped adults. The landlord has refused them admission. For the staff themselves to patronise the pub without concern seems to me quite extraordinary. They should not rest until with the residents they have preferably educated the landlord and his customers but alternatively shown a determination to expose such a barrier to the integration of the residents into the community. In any case, the joint efforts of staff and residents in a venture of this sort will be beneficial to their own relationships. Growing up with stigma is not necessarily the lot of people in residential establishments. It can only be minimised if staff are prepared to acknowledge it emotionally in the first place.

Moving into a home or residential school may make the problem that faced the resident before ten times greater, as many aspects of it now have to be lived with in the context of the pressures of the group.

Developing social skills

Living at home in the community, or indeed living to the full in a residential unit based in the community, demands a minimum level of social skills. These include the ability to speak on the telephone, to travel by bus or train, to check change in a shop, to use the post office and to buy clothes. Not all residents will have these skills. At a different level they may need to have a bank account, to know how to conduct themselves at interview, to budget, to learn to cope with social occasions, especially when mixing with the opposite sex, and to be able to enjoy a meal in a restaurant. Social skills not acquired as part of the earlier developmental process are less likely to come naturally following admission to a residential home. Opportunities may be lessened, and failure in some activities may result in ridicule.

Leroy, a personable 14-year old West Indian boy, would never go on a bus on his own. There seemed no reason for this, until it was realised that, on reaching his destination, he was unable to find the right bus for the return journey because he could understand neither the figures nor the letters on the indicator. On some occasions he had previously found himself being taken all over London, having got on the wrong bus, was railed against by the conductor for having no money, and became worried and angry. Leroy never let the other boys know about his problem, and he led an isolated existence in the home, fearful of joining in any game except football. With staff help, very privately and using a set of small, numbered cards, he was eventually enabled to find his way to a limited number of destinations and to make the return journey on his own without distress.

Vera could not get a job. When I witnessed her performance at interview it was not surprising. Role-play, often quite hilarious, was the answer. Vera improved her self-control and her ability to listen, practised being interviewed and shortly afterwards obtained employment. She attributed her success to her role-play sessions.

Residents often need to work at their social skills away from the group. It feels safer that way. Acute embarrassment is experienced by people unable to conduct themselves as one of the crowd in everyday exchanges with other people and with their environment. The vulnerability of young children, mentally handicapped people, physically handicapped people and elderly citizens is often apparent. Other residents may need assistance and feel their social inadequacies even more intensely.

Increasing trust
Helping residents to develop their social skills requires staff to increase their trust in them, especially in respect of handling money, encouraging them to be truthful and honest, and in managing their own time. The difficulties are enormous in working with some resident groups, but we hold back personal development and impede the social work task by not taking every opportunity to allow residents to test themselves in these areas. How else will they learn? Routine in residential establishments is important, but it may also create an artificial rhythm, out of step with the way time is managed elsewhere and creating an unhealthy dependency on the clock. More or less skilfully, most of us manage our time boundaries, learning or not learning as a result of our mistakes. Residents must, therefore, be given some flexibility in respect of times for meals, getting up and going to bed, and returning after an outing. Few of us miss a meal, are grumbled at or are made to feel bad if we get out of line with the rest of the household over this question of time. In the most relaxed living groups, these are not considered to be problems. Concern and communication prevent acrimony. While there are understandably constraints in residential homes and schools, I would suggest that a certain rigidity creeps in over the management of time for which there is no rationale other than the sanctity of the routine and the convenience of staff.

Why, I ask, do residents feel the need to be untruthful? They fear punishment and the loss of privileges, both of which provide a shaky foundation for living and working together. Each time a resident is able to be open and honest and as a result to be responded to, if not by acceptance of his or her actions, at least by understanding and the absence of sanctions, we lay the foundation for change. If our experience of telling the truth results in pain and deprivation, dishonesty will become a predictable pattern of behaviour. Staff reaction to minor misdemeanours in a comparatively closed group is more important than we suppose. Each exchange has the potential to drive in further the wedge between the cared for and the care giver, or to make telling the truth less traumatic. Punishment may satisfy the staff member. Working with the incident within the context of open communication will usually be more helpful to the resident in the long run.

Money, of course, is the focal point for deviousness and mistrust. Trust with money, as indicated in Chapter 1, only comes from handling money. Wasting money is part of growing up. Young people particularly will need help with this, they will need advice about budgeting and assistance with saving. Mistakes will occur as part of their experimentation. Adults must continue to trust, they must continue to take risks, with money and in other areas of human exchange and activity. When we withdraw trust we withdraw the possibility of growth through trust.

Many comments in the preceding paragraphs point to the importance of creating for residents opportunities for the demonstration of responsible behaviour, for example in helping to receive a newcomer into the home or being trusted with money. I use the word 'creating' advisedly in the knowledge that in many homes staff are inclined to be suspicious, not to trust and not to assume a link between 'being a resident' and 'responsible behaviour' as we would between being a friend or being a colleague and responsible behaviour. We therefore start by viewing residents differently. Sometimes, of course, residents are not responsible, and have to have their movements, behaviour and actions watched with extreme care in the way that adults would watch over a young child. If this continues, however, gradually permeating the whole of residents' lives, then they are being prepared for institutionalised living. Hence the value of developing alternative strategies on every possible occasion. Even when a host of other problems seemingly remains unsolved, the chance to show responsible behaviour is an essential part of later being able to manage life in the community.

This does mean the staff taking risks, and allowing residents to take risks, in a manner not always associated with living in residential care. One weakness of present approaches is the tendency to collude with the traditional institutional practice of over-protecting residents, often for very good, apparent reasons. The time has come to break out of this, helping residents to operate far more at the boundaries of personal responsibility, pushing individuals progressively, as agreed and where appropriate, to become involved in making decisions about their own lives and to manage additional areas of their lives.

Risk taking by an individual member of staff, or even a small staff group, is dangerous. In working at the boundaries there is inevitably failure as well as success and this may be viewed by others as 'negligence', 'carelessness' or 'mismanagement'. Questions will be asked. Staff will feel guilty, angry or let down. For this reason I return to the importance of establishing aims and objectives for every home, and care plans for each resident, both providing broad guidelines agreed by practitioners and managers about the particular approaches to residents and their lives. Risk taking must become a joint responsibility because, while a willingness to share the credit is always apparent when it is successful, there is a likelihood that an individual member of staff will be unfairly blamed when risk taking goes wrong. This fear, within all residential practitioners, ensures that many residents operate from a safe haven and well within the boundaries of their potential.

Enjoying the present
Just as disturbed and delinquent children need to make educational achievements, and adults need to be successful in obtaining acceptable employment or a satisfying occupation, so residents need to enjoy the present. It is part of the residential social work task to facilitate this. In this quest residents do not differ from the rest of the population. All the time residents are 'cases', are being assessed, discussed, transferred, 'treated' and regarded as different, (the processes sometimes stretching over many years) they are conscious, despite the preoccupations of others with their behaviour, disability or distress, of the stage in their lives that they have reached: as children, as adolescents, as young adults, as middle-aged people or as elderly people. As one youngster said to me: 'Having all these problems means like they don't want to let you go on living until they are all sorted out'.

Residents see and know what is happening to their friends, their peers and their families and they are aware of what they should be doing, what they would like to be doing and what they should be allowed to do in order to enjoy the present to the full. We may not agree with other people's perception of enjoyment. We may not agree with the residents' perception of enjoyment. What we must not do (in the absence of violence, vandalism, self-destruction or major law-breaking) is to turn this perception into pathology, reacting with punishment, additional controls, more 'treatment' or the further justification of our decision for having admitted a person to residential care or for keeping that person there.

Many people reasonably respected in the community – teachers, social workers and lawyers included – get drunk at parties or in their own homes. They may even take drugs occasionally or have casual sex with a friend or neighbour. People in the community live out their lives from a value base substantially different from that of a decade ago. In the case of both adults and young people, provided they are on time for work or school, provided their jobs are not affected, nobody writes anything down about them in a file. They are not reprimanded. In most instances their leisure pursuits are never known. The activities mentioned, perhaps for a larger number than we dare admit, are some of the ways in which people seek relaxation in order to enjoy the present. We must avoid taking over too much of another person's life merely because that person lives in a residential establishment.

A resident's band of enjoyment is narrow. Care givers often take too seriously the need to control, to prescribe, to limit, to condemn and to censure in areas of pleasure and recreation perfectly acceptable in today's moral and social climate. For a young person to stay at an all-night party is not, these days, unusual. It may not be to everybody's taste and it may fill some adults with apprehension, but it is not a crime and should not be punished. To expect a young person to return to the residential home just at the point when most of the other guests are arriving at a party imposes an intolerable burden, giving cause for bitter resentment of 'in care' status. The primary concerns should be that he or she returns safely, telephones if the return is to be much later than previously agreed, enjoys him or herself, is able to do so without getting into conflict with the law, is responsible enough not to get pregnant by accident or to get someone else pregnant, has worked out a means of getting home without being put at risk, and is able to fulfil the next morning's commitments. If young residents can be helped to see the importance of acting in this way they are really learning. Nothing is learned from being shouted at, threatened or inappropriately sanctioned. Adult counselling about the most suitable night of the week for such enjoyment, or even whether it is wise to go at all, would seem the best way to engage in dialogue with youngsters so that they are able to share, to be honest, to learn from mistakes and to avoid disastrous consequences from their actions. This is part of growing up, a part that residential staff are in a unique position to give assistance with, and not to over-control.

The residential home itself must become a place for greater enjoyment of the present, not only in the very traditional ways that local people offer 'entertainment' to residents, but in ways parallel to the activities of people in their own homes. One of the happiest tales I have heard recently came from a home for elderly people. The residents decided they wanted to hold a barbecue, were encouraged and assisted by the staff group to invite all their friends and relatives, and made a delightful and potent punch under the direction of an octogenarian for many years in the hotel trade. Everybody possible gave a hand in the preparations, and the event was a huge success. The milkman came, and the chiropodist, the minibus driver and his family and the man from the local newsagent's. All residents slept on until noon the next day, and not an upset stomach was reported! It was a night to remember and a party in which residents participated in much the same way as they would have done in their own homes as part of an extended family.

I recall from my own experiences so many simple happenings that 'broke all the rules' and upset routines but enhanced the quality of relationships between residents and between residents and staff: going out for long night walks in the hot summer just because it felt so good to be out at that time; having the wedding reception for two members of staff at the assessment centre where they worked with everybody involved; making curried dishes at midnight because a group of youngsters, mostly West Indians, returning from an evening out had witnessed an accident and wanted to talk, or merely needed time to unwind; and acting spontaneously in a manner that prevented rules, regulations and routine becoming sacred cows. Within a well thought out philosophy of care, the fears of staff that things will 'get out of hand' and chaos reign have no foundation in practice. The reverse is true. Opportunities to participate to the full in the fun activities of today make the inevitable daily constraints of residential living bearable, less apparent and non-destructive.

The home as a base for other activities
These in-house experiences are important but, both for those destined to live out their lives in a group setting, and as part of the growing up and growing away of those who will eventually leave residential care, the home or school must as often as possible be used as a base for other activities. It is better for a boy to join a football club in the community than for well motivated staff to encourage the residents to form a team at the home; better for a handicapped person to join a local evening class in a nearby school than for paid or voluntary workers to run classes in the home.

Tensions may arise in any establishment because it becomes the centre for too much: eating, sleeping, working and playing, and all with the same people. Each time individuals reach out to the community and make a successful link, they lessen their contribution to the dynamics and possible tensions of the home, and make themselves accessible to new social and emotional exchanges where every mood and the most vulnerable sides of the personality often remain unexposed, thereby strengthening their more acceptable characteristics. Sometimes we may know too much about residents for them to thrive. They may still need us in weaker moments, but the major part of 'living' will be elsewhere.

Developing personal relationships
It is the task of care givers to facilitate the growth of satisfying relationships, both inside and outside the establishment. I include here especially the hard-to-like residents, out to convince everybody that they are unwanted and unlovable people yet carrying within them the desire and hope of being special, of being loved as individuals and of finding somebody to love.

The inner isolation of many people in residential care is extreme. Many of the devices we employ to combat this can only ever be part of the solution. Residents are seeking permanency in a residential world of change. They are seeking an individual experience where attention and affection have to be shared. They are seeking someone whose ability to accept them, to tolerate them, to want to be with them is just that much more than care staff are in a position to respond to. Many anxieties within the individual, within the group and within the home may stem from this. It is significant that an individual resident who is able to share an experience or an outing with a single member of staff is usually at his or her most relaxed and communicative at this time. Returned to the group, the euphoria may be sustained for a while, although it is not unnatural for anger or depression to take over as the individual becomes conscious of the impermanence of the experience and of not being as he or she would like to be, special to someone for life.

Carson McCullers writes about 12-year old Frankie:

> Frankie had become an unjoined person who hung around in doorways and she was afraid ... she was an *I* person who had to walk around and do things for herself. All other people had a *we* to claim, all others except her'.[2]

There are many unjoined people in residential care and a primary task, perhaps *the* primary task, is to enable *I* people to become *we* people.

Residential staff cannot respond alone to the emotional needs of all the people living in their homes and schools. Fulfilling the needs of one resident may be at the expense of another. Only by making the walls of our establishments permeable to a degree rarely envisaged will we be able to hope for the right emotional exchanges. Often we insist on our right to know too much about residents. We do not allow them their secrets and their intrigues. Relationships cannot develop. Intrigue is a part of life frequently denied to residents who must have relationships open to examination, and sometimes approval.

Dawn lived in a girls' hostel, and had been looked after by many competent and caring residential social workers over the years. She was a strange, inward-looking, institutionally deviant 15-year old, an unjoined person, already on the spiral leading to ultimate rejection by the group, both staff and girls. Then, while working part time, she met Syd who was 52 years of age. For the next 18 months Dawn and Syd broke all the hostel rules and argued their way out of every tight corner. 'Conference opinion' stressed the need for the relationship to be discouraged and a CHE was put forward as an alternative placement. But the power of the relationship was greater than the power of the conference participants.

One day a long while after I picked Dawn up at the bus stop and drove her a few miles into town. Syd had died. They had lived together for four years. She had stayed on in the small cottage that he had left her in his will. Dawn appeared more outgoing; she seemed relaxed in spite of sadness at her recent loss. Dawn came alive when she met Syd. He became her 'key worker'. It was he who bullied the hostel, pleaded, cajoled and took the role of advocate when transfer to a CHE was being mooted.

Robert Pirsig poses the question: ' ... what do they really know of *kind*ness who are not *kin*?'[3] Syd was not at first kin to Dawn in the true sense, but he represented something that a residential social worker could rarely hope to give, a certainty born of one individual for another, concern that went beyond the working hours of the staff members and their holiday arrangements, the interests of the group and the policy of the department.

A resident must be allowed, indeed encouraged, to find somebody outside the establishment who will act as an emotional anchor. Although more prickly in content, the quality of Dawn's communication inside the hostel improved considerably after she had met Syd. She was operating from a position of security: she had become a *we* person.

When as a resident you are anxious or feeling oppressed, when you are the underdog, even when you are in the wrong, the greatest need is for someone who believes in you completely. At such times, a member of staff in role, endeavouring to accommodate a number of conflicting loyalties, may be of limited value to the resident. This is often difficult for us to accept, but as Liz Ward reminds us: '...for the person who has experienced massive failed relationships, professional niceties are unlikely to have much weighting'.[4]

Acknowledging the sexuality of residents

Residents are sexual beings with the range of curiosities, needs and frustrations common to the rest of the population. Their awareness may be heightened because of the physical proximity of other residents and the intimate nature of group living, inclining them towards homosexual or heterosexual behaviour.

Children, adolescents and adults in the community manage their sexuality in a variety of ways: siblings experiment as part of growing up; young people find opportunities for sexual exchanges in comfortable and relaxed surroundings, if only when other members of the family are out for the evening or by coming home from school during the day while their parents are at work; those who masturbate may do so in the privacy of their own rooms; and most adults have a freedom of movement that allows them to control much of their sexual lives, either inside or outside marriage.

Residents are immediately at a disadvantage. Privacy is at a premium, they are sometimes forced into subterfuges in order to satisfy basic urges, and sex too often becomes a furtive act disassociated from the warmth of a relationship, either permanent or temporary, and always in the fear of being caught. Too easily frustration turns to violence and intermittent sexual encounters provide nothing of the gentle stimulation, intensity of positive feeling and subsequent relaxation experienced by those fortunate enough to find the right partner. Instead, sex becomes something to ridicule, to make coarse remarks about, to regard as dirty, to endeavour to deny and, above all, to hide from watchful care givers.

In matters of sexuality most residents remain our prisoners. In Chapter 1 I suggested that examples of good practice over the last decade, while having many merits, have not in any way gone far enough in helping to liberate the people they are there to serve. The sexual liberation of residents has hardly begun.

Models of adulthood

Children in residential homes and schools grow up to become fathers and mothers of a new generation. Part of our task is to present them with the best possible models of adulthood, bearing in mind that within five years some of the 14-year olds in our care will be fathers and mothers to one or more children. Even the most hardened delinquent and the most violent and disruptive adolescents, locked up for months at a time, may become parents shortly after leaving care. I have no sense that we take this fundamental truth seriously.

There are at least two areas to consider: firstly what we are able to provide ourselves; and secondly what others have to offer. Ideally, our every action should be a model of adult–child contact, with a great deal of touching noticeable in our exchanges with children and young people; with an absence of threatening looks or gestures; with constant anticipation of need; with frequent interpretation of incidents; and with explanation of events yet to come. Young residents will watch carefully our ways of behaving with children of all ages, storing up consciously and unconsciously models for the future. Our performances in this respect do not always stand close scrutiny. It may be salutary to remember that everything that we are heard to say or seen to do to a child is a licence for children and young people in care to say and do similar things to their own offspring at some future date. Most parents draw heavily on their own experiences of being parented in bringing up their children. People who have spent the early part of their lives in care are no different.

It would seem right to expose our young residents as frequently as possible to ordinary adult–child relationships. Some children and young people in care may have very damaging experiences to correct in their perceptions of how adults should behave. A number will have grown up emotionally, physically and sexually abused. An important part of the social work task is to think deeply about the sort of parents they will become, perhaps in a very short while, and to take the most active steps possible to prepare them for the event. As we know, children in care often become the parents of children in care.[5]

I am reminded of a 10-year old boy brought up in residential care, taken to the home of a part-time worker. On entering the lounge of her semi-detached house he asked: 'Is this your group room?'

Some people move into a residential setting as a permanent alternative to living in their own homes. Sometimes this is known prior to admission. In other instances, a later decision is made. As residents, permanent or temporary, people will benefit from the work subsumed under the social work tasks outlined in this chapter. Through these a great deal may be accomplished, in helping to overcome earlier difficulties and in the encouragement of as near normal an existence as possible.

Preparing to leave care

For those who will eventually be leaving residential care, at 18 years or later in life, the tasks assume even greater importance. Unless they have in large measure been grappled with, the resident remains at risk. Preparation for leaving care therefore begins at the point of admission. Over the months or years, residents are either strengthened as staff work with them on the identified tasks or become increasingly disturbed, delinquent or distressed as they drift through care without purpose or direction.

Progress will rarely be uniform, with numerous setbacks making staff uncertain about the value of their efforts and fearful for the future of the residents. As the time approaches to leave the residential home or school, and especially when worthwhile work has been undertaken with them, residents will often regress to earlier patterns of behaviour, testing once again the concern of the care givers and expressing anxieties about their ability to survive away from the protected environment in which they have been living. I feel sure that people's success in sheltered accommodation or independent living is directly related to the quality of the detailed work carried out during their time in residential care.

4 Staff Learning, Supervision and Consultancy

Most members of staff take up their appointments in residential homes and schools with little experience of social work, with no understanding of the dynamics of group living and with minimal awareness of resident and staff potential for the display of unexpectedly strong feelings and emotions.

Reference has already been made to the weight of the problems residents may bring with them on moving into care, to the initial confusion they may feel in living with a group of unfamiliar people and to the need for staff responses that show a willingness to share the burdens residents are carrying.

Problems arise for staff, too, as they seek to resolve questions relating to the exercise of power, authority and control; to their fears in the face of hostility or depression; to the demands of colleagues operating from different value bases; to the feelings of inadequacy in helping residents overcome major handicaps; to the impact of their own sexuality; to finding alternative ways of working; and to the possible erosion of self-images comfortably built over time. As noted in Chapter 3, residents often compete in each other's presence for a worker's attention and emotional investment, an additional factor in appreciating staff need for self-management of a high order.

Responding to staff stress

Residential homes are increasingly being staffed by sensitive, thoughtful, caring, fragile and vulnerable people. Demonstrations of sensitivity and acknowledgements of their own vulnerability are essential staff qualities in working with residents. Given a supportive framework many staff are well equipped to offer a service to those in their homes and residential schools, such a framework not only providing a vehicle for the examination and clarification of the stressful aspects of the job, but affording occasions for the positive reinforcement of what appear the best ways of working with residents.

For staff to wrestle in isolation with their vulnerability, fears and sense of inadequacy is debilitating, unproductive and even destructure. After a year or two staff may often seek other employment in anger, frustration or despair. We must reverse this trend, the exodus being not unconnected with the poverty of opportunities for learning, supervision and consultancy we find in some local authority and voluntary establishments.

Types of training

I do not intend to dwell here on the formal learning available to staff, namely in-service training, preparation for the Certificate in Social Service and training for the Certificate of Qualification in Social Work. Open to development in a variety of ways, these remain the basic qualifications to which staff should aspire. Rather I am thinking of *individual supervision, group supervision, in-house training* and *consultancy*, all of which I have been engaged in during recent years.

Feelings and emotions

First, however, I refer readers to the diagram overleaf. This sets out for both residents and care givers the forces at work at the moment of any behavioural exchange: feelings, emotions, physical sensations and past experiences. Without considerable understanding of what contributes to our own behaviour and what contributes to the behaviour of residents, we have much less chance of reducing their stress, minimising our own anxiety or modifying residents' behaviour. Staff must be enabled to increase this understanding by means of the regular analysis and consistent monitoring of their approaches to practice. Without a forum for staff development, there is less likelihood of working successfully on many of the tasks outlined in the previous chapter. While not denying the importance of spontaneity in relationships between staff and residents, too easily our responses remain at the level of 'raw' exchanges, and of limited value to residents.

Arnold makes a helpful distinction between feelings and emotions:

> Emotions may be like feelings in that both indicate that something is agreeable or attractive, and somthing else disagreeable and unattractive. But they are unlike feelings in that emotions are going out to some object while feelings merely indicate our reactions to a particular aspect of an object or a situation. Feelings can vary while the emotion remains the same: anger expressed without any fear of retaliation may be rather pleasant; anger unexpressed is extremely unpleasant. Requited love is

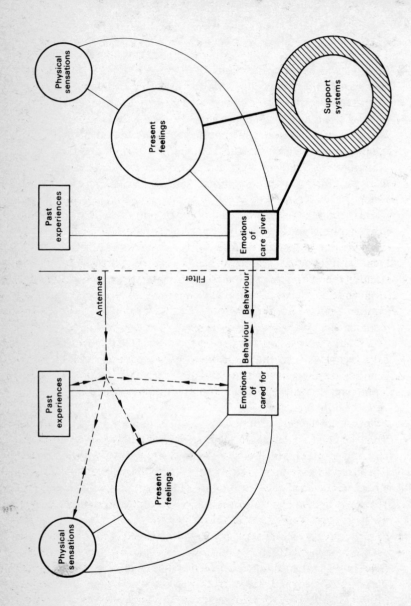

pleasant, love unrequited, most disagreeable. If we agree that feelings include pleasantness and unpleasantness, then we must conclude that they are distinct from emotions ... Emotion always focuses on the object, while feeling reveals my momentary state of mind.[1]

The same distinction is being made in respect of residential work. Feelings indicate our reactions to particular aspects of objects, processes or incidents while emotions arise directly from the results of human exchanges, past or present. Nevertheless, and particularly in close living groups, unpleasant feelings which in other circumstances would pass as trivial may suddenly act as a springboard for intense emotional interaction.

Supervision and consultancy are primarily concerned with feelings and emotions, with the whole mind–body experiences which bring about the admission of residents; which block easy integration into the living group; which may prevent them from leaving care; which motivate so much of the action in residential settings; which, to varying degrees, act as barriers to staff involvement with the 'real' task; and which we frequently fail to understand in their complexity. Sometimes staff are operating at a feeling level while being out of touch with the emotional burdens, past and present, being borne by residents. On other occasions, they overreact to the behaviour of residents, for example to the normal developmental pangs of an adolescent or the early admission-to-care feelings of an elderly person, either by ascribing to them significance beyond their meaning or, alternatively, by behaving destructively because of their own emotional conflicts.

Physical sensations
I turn briefly to physical sensations. Not without reason in ordinary conversation do we use the phrases 'trembling with anxiety', 'flushed with anger' or 'sick with fear'. The physical expression of emotional turmoil is common among residents, as a manifestation of both their inner conflicts and their bewilderment in making sense of the processes and pressures in which they are caught up. Staff, too, will react to residents from a physical base, from what they are currently experiencing within their bodies, for example when timorously trying to calm a violent adolescent or enraged by an outburst of personal abuse from a mentally ill person. Extreme fatigue, headaches, sore throats or general nervousness may occur after prolonged periods of living and working with a group of very disturbed residents. Boris Pasternak comments on the harm

resulting from the 'constant systematic duplicity' of our lives:

> Your nervous system isn't a fiction, it's part of your physical
> body, and your soul exists in space and is inside you, like
> the teeth in your head. You can't keep violating it with im-
> punity...[2]

Controlled response to residents

In this as in other facets of our lives the personalities of staff
member and resident 'do not stand opposed to each other as two
external facts that do not meet and cannot be compared'.[3] Both
cared for and care giver have a range of emotions, past experiences,
physical sensations and present feelings which they bring to any
exchange. Yet there is a difference for staff, resulting from the
'filter system' of the individual care giver which, to some degree,
tempers words and actions. On the one hand, as the diagram
shows, we feed into the filter our background, our training, our
role, our feelings and our emotions, the climate of the establishment and indeed our whole beings; on the other hand, it encourages
us to put out 'antennae' in the direction of residents' past
experiences, physical sensations, present feelings and emotions
with a view to increasing understanding and offering help.

The smooth operation of the filter as an aid to meeting the needs
of residents will be a reflection of the care givers' awareness of their
own feelings and emotions, and of the nature of the support systems
which they *have* and which they *feel*. If staff are asked what they
mean by support many will be hesitant in their replies, having
inadequately formulated concepts of social work supervision and
the nature of consultancy. Most will need to be taught to use professional support systems, and some may be reluctant to commit
themselves to the unknown. Therefore staff must feel personally
rewarded soon after they elect to participate in formal supervisory
processes.

Individual supervision

Few homes have developed individual supervision to the extent that
it is found in fieldwork. Administrators, external managers and
senior practitioners sometimes seem unwilling to allocate time and
to make the necessary emotional investment in establishing it as a
tool vital to the residential social work task. I am convinced of its
importance.

Learning on the job entails increasing and refining knowledge,
applying it wisely and improving workers' ability to handle both

their own feelings and emotions, and those of the residents. Learning is ultimately an individual responsibility and an individual experience. Sometimes it is not without stress. George Wright has drawn up a useful checklist for supervisors, and in this he points to the need for supervisors to encourage a positive attitude towards learning from one's own experience; to develop a relationship within which staff feel safe enough to recall their actions and the motivation for their actions; and to increase the capacity of staff to tolerate the expression of feelings by residents as well as controlling their own emotional reactions.[4] Only in residential settings are workers so completely surrounded by their learning material all the time; is it so rooted in personal experiences; and created by them in every decision, every interaction.

In the previous chapter I suggested that the need for a definition or redefinition of boundaries is constantly occurring in any non-punitive approach by staff determined to use purposefully the day-to-day events, important and unimportant, concerning the individual or happening within the group. An essential aspect of individual supervision is the ability of the supervisor and the member of staff to maximise the worker's strengths and skills as he or she responds to the multiplicity of incidents that take place in swift succession within these ever-changing boundaries. This is one reason why the personal support strand of supervision, as opposed to the managerial and educational aspects, is often the most difficult to handle. Staff may be too vulnerable even to acknowledge that they have difficulties, or they may welcome the opportunity to castigate themselves for the inadequacy they feel. Neither of these is helpful. A worker's strengths must be acknowledged whenever possible. While weaknesses should not be denied, it is on strengths and skills that we build.

As in all relationships, the supervisory one has to be worked at. There has to be commitment. Supervisors need training. With increasing numbers of qualified staff in residential homes, there will be an expectation of continuing the patterns of supervision established in training. Residential social workers have a right to the fulfilment of that expectation.

Group supervision

I have often found that, in the absence of a framework for individual supervision, or as a preparation for it, group supervision is valued by staff members. It is frequently less threatening to a young member of staff, is economical in the use of time, offers an open meeting place for focused discussion in a facilitating environment and may legitimately operate at a lower level of intellectual and emotional intensity in its early stages and as individuals accustom themselves to using the group process.

Group supervision does demand leadership skills in the senior staff member running the group, he or she does require an understanding of group dynamics, and there is a likelihood that the leader may feel threatened as the group gains momentum. In many ways it is more rewarding than work with individuals. A useful starting point is the discussion of a particular event, an unhappy occurrence or the management of routines, for example, getting up or mealtimes. Where community meetings are held, group supervision provides the means for making an analysis of what transpired. As group supervision progresses, the need to develop the personal support elements identified earlier will become apparent, the leader also having to give members of the group a joint learning experience which satisfies the needs of each individual.

The complexity of group supervision arises from a number of factors unique to residential social work: the response of individual members of staff to residents is often visible to colleagues; the residents are usually the clients of all the workers; the group leader is part of the process; and frequently the leader's own approach to practice is seen by members of the group.

In-house training
Before moving to the question of consultancy I wish to refer to the value of in-house training. Traditionally, individual members of staff have been sent away for training in order to gain professional qualifications, and this concept of training has also been established over the years for short courses. The latter, on a regional or national basis, of course still have their place in providing space for staff away from their usual setting, in promulgating ideas and in allowing staff to make some measure of their standards vis-à-vis those of colleagues in neighbouring local authorities or in the voluntary sector. Such training programmes are, however, often costly, involving overnight accommodation and considerable travelling expenses.

More and more I find local authorities providing in-house training programmes as a response to special needs: how to deal with incontinence; how to establish a framework for individual supervision; how to help residents help themselves; how to plan for leaving care; how to work with very young children; how to tackle problems of alcoholism and drug abuse; how to improve communication within the home; how to work with outside agencies; how to respond to prospective foster parents; and so on. Such topics lend themselves to individual sessions or a series of seminars. They provide learning opportunities, stimulate discussion and remind staff that the problems they experience can be eased by a concentration of thought, new knowledge, clarification of the essential components of a difficulty and reference to practice handbooks.

The advantages of in-house training are that the tutor is able to see personally the problems being encountered and is teaching a group with many common experiences. It differs from consultancy in that the tutor has a more closely defined brief, is more concerned with formal teaching and learning, and the responsibility for beginnings and endings has more of an educational than an emotional base.

The place of consultancy

Consultancy may be used to good effect by residential establishments in a variety of ways. Preferably as an addition to individual or group supervision but sometimes as an alternative to group supervision (where skills and circumstances do not allow its development), consultancy may provide a rather more neutral forum for the analysis of events, for identifying and helping to unravel the complexities of group living, and for putting into perspective some of the painful incidents likely from time to time to rock the foundations of any home or school where staff work intensively with groups of residents.

I have been engaged in three types of consultancy: having an open-ended commitment to a large CHE, working there for a full day weekly or fortnightly; helping staff over a three-month period as they prepare for the formal review of their home by senior management (later discussed in Chapter 5); and providing short term crisis intervention following a particularly destructive episode in the life of a home. All have their place in enabling staff to maintain their work performance by increasing their skills, heightening their self-awareness, reducing tension and raising their level of understanding.

Confidentiality is a central feature of consultancy. There is no management responsibility – although there is an overall responsibility *to* management – and what transpires between the consultant and the individual and the consultant and the group must not be fed back to senior staff of the home or to external managers except in very general terms about trends, fears or attitudes. This encourages a greater freedom of expression, and the exchange of ideas and feelings. In individual work the staff members know that their opinions, weaknesses and mistakes will not be made public. They will often feel safe enough to reveal intimate details about their past or present which must be aired and understood if they are to obtain optimal success in work with residents. For a manager to be entrusted with too much of the staff members' personal histories, fears and fantasies would sometimes make the job untenable. He or she would frequently be bound to act on newly-acquired knowledge, but in the long term would not necessarily be helping either the staff members or the residents.

I should like to propose the more frequent use of consultancy as a method of crisis intervention at the level of the establishment. The reaction to a major incident involving a member of staff in a home or residential school – whether this relates to theft, negligence, violence or a sexual allegation – is often brusque and unqualified. Suspensions, warnings, new procedures or resignations may follow rapidly. Sometimes the hurt person is reinstated when nothing is proved, and sometimes resigns rather than become the centre of attention, even when not 'guilty'. Whether the individual goes or stays, whether proved guilty or not, in a senior or a junior position, life cannot go on, either for staff or residents, as if nothing had happened.

Re-establishing the equilibrium of an establishment may well be facilitated by involving an external consultant at times when supicion is at its height, when staff tensions are beginning to get in the way of the work with residents or, in the case of the most people-centred local authorities, where they seek constantly to heal rather than to destroy, thereby offering a model for staff to pass on in supporting residents in crisis.

A case example

As an illustration, I would like to describe a piece of work in which I was engaged last year, probably the most satisfying and most satisfactory I have undertaken. It took place in a children's home.

The large, converted house at 58 College Avenue was a short-stay home for 20 children, mainly in the younger age range. Of the 12 staff three were men, the head of home being female, and the deputy, male. The staff group was young, few workers being over

26 years of age. Undoubtedly this was a home working to a high standard of child care practice with the adults committed to working sensitively with the children and in depth.

Then tragedy struck. A four-year old boy, recently fostered, described innocently to his new parents how Andy had 'played' with him when he lived in the children's home, sometimes sucking his penis. Andy was the deputy head of home.

Events moved swiftly. The little boy's foster parents alerted the social worker, senior management was informed and the matter became too serious for the police not to be notified. They took immediate action: two detectives arrived at the children's home unannounced and the three male members of staff were asked to go along to the police station for questioning. It must have seemed a nightmare, and Andy was suspended for a period of several weeks while further enquiries were made and decisions arrived at.

Feelings within the home inevitably ran high, the children asked questions about the disappearance of a key member of staff and an impenetrable dark cloud was left hanging over Andy's future as he waited in torment for the outcome. Prosecution, dismissal or resignation seemed the strongest possibilities as a result of the youngster's allegation.

One of the other male workers, Clive, obviously distressed by the suspension of his colleague and friend, asked for an additional day off but never returned to duty. He took an overdose after posting a letter of confession to the head of the home. In this he said that there had been a case of mistaken identity and that he, Clive, had been responsible for interfering with young David, a statement that made those working inside and outside the home think about their initial responses to Andy following the accusation, about their images of the staff member who had decided to take his life, and about an allegation the previous year that had eventually come to nothing.

And so Andy was reinstated, resuming his duties as deputy head of home. The matter seemed closed, with what was probably a vain hope that the incident would soon be forgotten. But David's words lingered powerfully; Andy had to carry the pain of his isolation during the period of his suspension; some members of staff, both internal and external, may have regretted their first, hasty judgements; Andy somehow had to manage his reintegration into the home; and an uneasy atmosphere was bound to prevail on his return to duty.

Such was the strength of Andy's resolve, I feel sure that both personally and professionally he would have rebuilt his confidence over time single-handed. This may, however, have been too much to ask, and there remained other members of staff: some who had stood beside Andy; others who had been suspicious; one or two who had been uninvolved; and newcomers more or less aware of the incident as a skeleton in the cupboard.

When I was asked by the training officer, residential services, to go to 58 College Avenue a few months after the disturbance, most of the older children had moved on, and my task was to work with the staff group, to explore their feelings and, if possible, to open up the question of David's allegations, Andy's suspension and Clive's suicide, breaking into the real fear that they would forever become part of the myth and legend of the home. I was given a free hand to work in the way I chose, with the assurance that I could regard as confidential, either to the individual or the group, anything that surfaced.

It was important to think carefully about how best to proceed. I decided to offer individual interviews to all who were in post at the time of the incident, including Andy and the head of the home. Newcomers to the staff, about six in number, were seen as a group. It seemed important to gain a comprehensive picture of fact and feeling, fantasy and opinion, before working with the staff as a whole.

Equipped, therefore, with substantial knowledge of 'how it happened' and about the intensity of the residual feeling, it was possible to plan a series of staff seminars as a vehicle for the primary task. These were offered under the broad headings of touch and sexuality; adolescent sexuality; basic values; adult feelings towards sexually abused children and their parents; and staff fears about the sexual side of their intimate contacts with children, space being created for members of the group to express themselves at their own pace and in safety. Andy helped the group considerably at the second meeting by giving in full, with great courage and no anger, his account of the events surrounding David and Clive. All had now heard the same story, myths were exploded and the rest of the group were released from their compulsive silence or the splinter-group discussion that had previously taken place.

At the end of my involvement with the home it was agreed that no good would come of perpetuating the story of the incident, members of the group expressed their willingness to allow the matter to 'fade' as a new group of residential social workers took up their appointments and the home continued its work by offering placements to nearby CQSW training courses.

Certainly over the weeks I sensed a feeling of relief in the group, and was subsequently able to move on to discuss the role of supervision as a way of helping young members of staff to deal more effectively with their own sexuality in the intimacies of group living, and with what some experience as the sexual attractiveness of children and young people.

I know of local authorities and residential homes where my task would have been much more difficult, if not impossible. At 58 College Avenue I felt a great deal of trust, moved into a staff group where the levels of honesty, commitment and enthusiasm were extraordinarily high, where the external manager was secure enough to hand over temporarily part of his responsibility, where the head of home and her deputy were able to set aside their roles during the 90-minute session, where an impressive personal effort was made to attend regularly, and where there was a belief in the exercise as a way of moving forward the work of the home.

I would not wish on any establishment the trauma experienced at 58 College Avenue. Few members of staff would have come out as unscathed as Andy in respect of future work performance. I feel, however, that he is now an even more sensitive manager and supervisor for that unwanted experience, one which in so many settings and in other circumstances could have destroyed him. As both participant and consultant I, too, learned a great deal.

Responding to extreme crisis

Crises will continue to occur in residential homes and schools. I would think that the deterrent effect of a heavy management response is at best limited. Human vulnerability does find its outlet in many guises, and residential establishments make visible people's frailty in respect of sexuality, strong feelings, minor delinquency or their propensity to violence perhaps more than in any other occupation. The dividing lines between personal and public, work and leisure, client and friend, appropriate and inappropriate and even legal and illegal are much less clearly defined.

Our responses to staff vulnerability – as managers, as supervisors, as consultants – affect not only the person on whom the spotlight falls at the moment of tragedy. Everything that the individual does or has done to him or her ripples through the home or school. Except for the most serious, premeditated or long-lasting episodes, perhaps we should always endeavour to give a second chance, looking in the mean time at the structural or supervisory imperfections that contributed to the expression of individual weaknesses.

5 A Strategy for Change

Over the years some social services departments have failed to set out their aims and objectives for people received into residential care, and then to see these through to a conclusion. Although we find, almost in isolation, valuable statements of intent, worthwhile policy documents and skilled practice, policy and practice are often disjointed rather than dovetailed, and the quality of life experiences offered to residents is consequently weakened to the extent that the two Ps are ill co-ordinated.

The need for statements of policy
It is not difficult to make policy statements about residential care to which most people of various political colours would subscribe. They are usually at a level of generality that does not imply responsibility for any particular course of action. It is, however, a fact that:

> Partly because of the tendency to provide answers in response to specific needs of different client groups, and partly as a result of piecemeal development, no fundamental philosophy exists upon which to base provision for all individuals needing care outside their own homes... The aims and objectives of particular establishments and their relationship with other services are often unstated, if not unknown, with the result that the role of staff, and the expectations of both staff and residents, are confused or lacking in specific purpose.[1]

I am sure that agencies should maintain statements of policy to be upheld throughout the agency, and many local authorities are now moving in this direction, drawing up guidelines for work with different client groups.

Problems arise, however, when policy is translated into practice. Detailed policy statements demand commitment if action is to flow from the words. They have resource implications and cannot be divorced from the politics in which we are all ensnared. If, for example, the policy of my local authority emphasises the need for delinquent boys to be cared for in small groups, I am likely to be embarrassed when, 12 years after the Children and Young Persons Act 1969, I still have a block school for 80 boys with no plans for dividing it into smaller units, or appear satisfied with having units housing 25 to 30 boys.

A policy statement is a reference point for development. Take two concepts that have already been mentioned, 'shared decision taking' and 'maximum independence'. If, as a head of home and in the spirit of agency policy, I encourage these ideas in practice, then I cannot be faulted, and indeed have a right to support from the homes manager, when the going gets rough. Alternatively, as a homes manager wishing to promote the same concepts I may want some way of challenging a head of home who is unwilling to move from an autocratic, over-protective regime. Here a policy statement is important.

Aims and objectives for each home

I would take this further, attaching to the policy of the agency a list of aims and objectives for each home, setting out unambiguously what it hopes to achieve, such aims having been arrived at jointly by the staff and external managers. Well-defined aims and objectives for each home allow the agency to develop a variety of specialised resources; enable reviews of establishments to take place (because only with a measuring rod in the form of written aims and objectives is it possible for reviews to be held satisfactorily); and provide the basis of a prospectus for all professional users of the establishment, for adult residents-to-be, for relatives, for parents and for young people old enough to appreciate a copy.

The prospectus, presented in a way that indicates opportunities for living and working together, should have a strong thread tying it to the policy of the agency.

Policy into practice

In translating policy into practice too often the gap becomes a gulf. It can be narrowed and, in the numerous homes and residential schools I visit, frequently it is being narrowed. There is, however, one possible split, that of intellectual as opposed to emotional acceptance of good practice. Few people are ever able to marry these completely, but the struggle to achieve this must be a primary goal, both for individual practitioners and for managers on behalf of those they supervise.

I have sketched a few ideas on the relationship between policy and practice because I feel that only against such a backcloth should we receive people into residential care, and thus enable local authorities to develop resources designed to meet the needs of particular groups of residents.

Residential establishments are influenced by a variety of factors, for example, the location and structure of the building; the composition of the resident group; the experience and enthusiasm of the staff; the leadership skills of the head of home; the quality of external management; the relationships between field and residential workers; and the political persuasion of the local authority.

The nature of change

These influences change over time, month by month and year by year, each holding back or moving forward the work of the home or school and having a direct effect on the daily lives of the residents. Establishments sometimes acquire a reputation as either 'good' or 'bad', built perhaps on the bitter experience of one field-worker from an area office whose client has run into difficulties, on a complaint to a councillor from a parent or relative, on the sustained, positive feedback following the discharge of residents, or on the rather superficial praise arising from a series of articles in a local newspaper. Whatever image is around at any time it is a picture that will remain for a while and be reflected in the type of applicants applying for staff vacancies, in the stability or high turnover of the staff group, and in the number of requests made by fieldworkers seeking admission for their clients. I can think of establishments engaged in very good work trying to live down incidents that occurred several years ago and of well-known, popular homes and schools where residents receive physical care and social work services of a poor standard.

How, therefore, is it possible to make more accurate statements about what is happening in an establishment, to measure the pulse of the resident group, to correct unhelpful trends, to reverse bad practice, and to enliven and enrich the work of the home or school in a way that is not destructively threatening to the head and the staff? It is the answers to these questions that we are seeking in this chapter.

Undoubtedly change can be a slow and painful process. Those who initiate it may attract hostility; those who are required to change have to face the possible rejection of routines and approaches to residents on which their individual ideas of good practice have been founded. For each group of staff there is a need for reassurance about the usefulness of change, bringing as it does personal and institutional disruption.

Yet in this fast-moving world change is inevitable. Merely to keep residents in step with the shifting norms of society staff must frequently examine the tasks associated with everyday care. To move beyond this in the hope of making some redefinition of residential care demands conceptual thought and personal resources of a high order.

Change: a painful process?

In 1967 Rosemary Dinnage and Mia Kellmer Pringle wrote:

> If even half of what is now clearly known were accepted with feeling and carried out with understanding by all, the picture of residential child care could be transformed . . . the immediate and major problem is to will the means to translate into action what is already known.[2]

Nine years later Hilary Prosser found it necessary to repeat these words, noting that:

> very little appears to have changed either in the nature of residential care itself in this country, or . . . in the findings of research which could itself inform policy and practice.[3]

Ron Walton underlined these comments in an article on research for practice,[4] all of which applies not only to the residential care of children, but with equal force throughout the work undertaken with other client groups.

It has only gradually been recognised that some skills, once highly esteemed, belong primarily to a former age, for example, the ability to supervise, single-handed if necessary, a large group of boys while they eat a meal in near-silence; the speed which ensures that all elderly or handicapped residents are up, dressed and with their beds made for breakfast at 8 am; or the organisation resulting in such a clinically clean and tidy establishment that it is never possible to be caught out by unexpected visitors. These outward signs of efficiency brought job satisfaction to heads of homes and members of staff groups. But as new primary skills have emerged they are no longer seen as the bench-marks of satisfactory residential care. For those whose status has depended on such visible evidence of expertise the threat is great. They ask themselves, and others ask around them: 'What skills will be demanded if we jettison those we seemingly have? Will other skills be found within an alternative framework of care?'. Many of the skills necessary for residential social work practice in the 1980s have already been identified. For some members of staff they present a challenge. Others, however, are overwhelmed by the magnitude of the changes demanded.

Of course, over time, extensive change has occurred within residential social work, and within individual establishments. Sometimes organised initiatives from homes staff acting collectively have brought about change, and, on rare but significant occasions, resident rebelliousness has achieved wonders. In the future there is little doubt that both staff and residents will increasingly have recourse to the law in their efforts to challenge decisions or maintain and improve standards. Change has also been brought about by a crisis when a committee of inquiry has made strong recommendations to a local authority. This happened, for example, in Salford in 1977. Following an allegation of ill-treatment at the assessment centre an independent inquiry was made into the care of the children living there. Among other recommendations the committee of inquiry made reference to the outmoded institutional practices and insensitive and harsh treatment of the children; and to the need for the social services committee to recognise that children in care should have rights, including the right to complain about ill-treatment.[5]

Such examples of change offer no model for the development of residential practice. Washington Irving once wrote:

> There is a certain relief in change, even though it be from bad to worse; as I have found in travelling in a stage coach, that it is often a comfort to shift one's position and be bruised in a new place.[6]

Haphazard change within residential care has often resulted in bruised people. There must be a better way.

Reviewing establishments
In some local authorities a system of reviewing establishments on a formal basis is being introduced as a regular feature of the work. Undeniably this may be regarded as a management tool but, more than this, it should be looked upon as part of the task which furthers the overall development of the home or school under scrutiny. Even the smallest home can benefit from such an enterprise.

I acknowledge that sometimes the review of an establishment will highlight gross defects, or even malpractice, and that there is no alternative to decisive action by management. Otherwise, a thorough assessment is as likely to bring to the surface a range of conditions for which external managers, officers and members, must be held jointly responsible. I refer, for instance, to the excessive use of agency staff, to the physical state of the building, to the number of unqualified staff in post, to admission procedures and to the level of support and supervision. In other words, it must be seen as a bipartite venture, with unsatisfactory replies to searching questions sometimes being the responsibility of the head of home and the staff, and on other occasions acknowledged as the result of deficiencies outside the home. Rarely will issues be as black and white as this, with most lending themselves to discussion and at least some degree of resolution as part of continuing development.

Reviews can also be stimulating. They provide a vehicle for approval and reinforcement of some of the excellent work to be found; they offer a regular method of examining needs and difficulties; and they help to expose weaknesses and to set goals as yet ill defined or unachieved. I feel there is no more successful way of bringing about controlled change, either within an individual establishment or as part of the policy development of a local authority eager to make the best of its resources in the service of residents.

Changing by stages

The process of change may be seen in four stages: *identification, realignment* or *replacement, development* and *evaluation*. It is not difficult for residents, practitioners and managers to identify unhelpful practice, for example a paucity of community links; review systems for individual residents that lack bite; aspects of residential care militating against the growth of the individual; or positive elements of group living that are being insufficiently exploited. As many members of staff and residents as possible should be involved with external managers in this process of *identification*. Sometimes coming together will bring about a clarification of previous misunderstandings and facilitate a shift of attitudes. This in turn may be enough for a *realignment* of thought and action that will result in more harmonious and purposeful living. Alternatively, some features of residential care may immediately be so unpalatable to all involved that some *replacement* of practice or policy is considered necessary.

Some issues are easy to pinpoint in a climate of open discussion. A conspiracy of silence may, however, surround many other aspects of the life of a home or residential school, with staff consciously or unconsciously resistent to replacing well-trodden paths. Winkling out the insidious or unsavoury features of an establishment may take considerable time.

Next comes the stage of *development*. Good ideas and statements of intent are not in themselves sufficient. The world is littered with abandoned good ideas, and statements of intent are made in abundance. Neither has value until carried forward to become an integral part of the development strategies of the agency. Development is the moment when change becomes painful, when tensions arise and when we seek, sometimes desperately, to justify the practices that we are endeavouring to change, hankering for a return to earlier and more comfortable routines. Supervision, consultation and support become particularly important at this time. Without them, many well thought out, sincerely launched and exciting formulations founder at the developmental stage, with ultimate chaos and embitterment. With them, however, change can be brought about and the practice of residential work edges forward a little.

The fourth stage, *evaluation*, focuses on the overall effect of new policy or practice, looks at the wider implications of such change and considers how the aims and objectives of the establishment have been brought nearer to fulfilment. Within this stage further questions of identification, realignment or replacement and development will emerge, thereby emphasising the never-ending dynamic quality of planned change.

The regular review of establishments followed through by determined management, both internal and external, can bring about change in a way that runs parallel to this four-stage process. Identification takes place at the first review; in some instances realignment or replacement must swiftly follow, but most change will be brought about between reviews in conjunction with management initiative and training facilities, the results of these efforts being seen at the point of evaluation. This forms part of the next review, change thereby becoming a built-in, rolling process punctuated by an annual or biennial review of the establishment.

In any exercise of this nature as many people as possible should be involved. We each see our individual worlds from very different perspectives, especially in moving backwards and forwards between fact and opinion.

There are many ways of establishing review procedures and local authorities will develop the criteria for evaluation in response to their own needs. A great deal will obviously depend upon the stage of development of the particular home, and the extent to which there is real engagement in the social work task, following through to a conclusion the policy of the agency. It is neither possible nor desirable to provide a blueprint, different geographical areas, different resident groups and different aims and objectives determining the most important areas for immediate scrutiny and evaluation. The checklist in the Appendix provides a basis for self-assessment and review.

A case example
The following example of a review of an old people's home is based on a locally developed set of evaluative criteria, but some of the areas covered in the Appendix are included, and additional ones are explored. The document was prepared by the Homes Manager in consultation with the senior staff of the home for consideration by the Director of Social Services who later held a 'home review' with the Assistant Director (Residential Services), the Staff Development Officer, the Homes Manager, the Head of Home and the Deputy Head of Home.

49 Bridge Walk, built in 1964, is a home reasonably well situated for local shops and is close to bus stops. There are 58 places made up of eight rooms with four beds, ten double rooms and six single rooms. The report read as follows:

1. THE BUILDING
1.1   Even though it was purpose-built there are a number of inherent design faults at 49 Bridge Walk which make the current care of residents more difficult than it would be in a building of recent construction. There are several major disadvantages:
1.1.1.   The split-level design means that 30 of our residents have to negotiate two short flights of steps, three steps to each flight. Of the 30 residents 18 are able to manage these on their own, but the other 12 require staff help.
1.1.2   The sprawling nature of the home means very long corridors and, in most cases, makes residents' rooms extremely remote from the general living areas which are concentrated at the main entrance to the building. This does not encourage residents to use their own rooms during the day because of the physical effort involved.
1.1.3   The large proportion of four-bedded and double rooms makes the creation of privacy and the maintenance of dignity almost impossible to achieve for the residents who occupy these rooms. There are no facilities for nursing sick residents, and this makes it particularly unpleasant for all who share multiple rooms. The use

of room dividers and ceiling hung curtaining around wash-hand basins would be an improvement.

1.1.4　The basic design of the toilets is poor and the provision in the main living area inadequate and badly sited. For day time use there are five toilets for the 58 residents. The situation might be alleviated by installing an additional toilet in the ground floor bathroom.

1.1.5　There is nothing homely about the design of the bathroom.

1.1.6　There is a lack of storage space both in the kitchen and in the home generally.

1.1.7　Residential staff accommodation is limited. There are two one-bedroomed flats which are used for sleeping-in purposes. For the past year one of these has been used by the local area office for social worker accommodation. The Head of Home has a flat at 17 Craven Way, about two miles down the road. She is a resident member of staff but still has to leave her home and family to do her share of on call duty at 49 Bridge Walk. The Deputy Head of Home and the Senior Assistant are both non-resident and this eases the burden on the accommodation. However, in the event of having to recruit new senior staff we are always seriously limited in the choice of candidate because of the lack of attractive accommodation.

1.2　We feel that urgent attention should be given to the planning of major improvements within the home to eliminate the problems listed. This should include the reduction of numbers to something like 40 so that a higher quality of care may be given.

2.　GROUNDS AND GARDENS

2.1　The sloping nature of the grounds does not encourage residents to make a great deal of use of them other than at the front entrance area. We feel that one or two parts of the garden such as the pond area could be improved so that, with encouragement, residents could obtain more enjoyment from them. The tightness of the site makes vehicle access difficult and we have very few parking areas. There appears little or nothing that can be done to improve this. The maintenance of the grounds is satisfactory with a visit by the peripatetic gardener once a week.

3.　POLICIES, PLANNING AND MONITORING PROCESSES

3.1　There is no clearly written operation policy for the establishment, although a senior management working party is due to report shortly with a view to establishing departmental guidelines for practice. The Head of Home is strongly committed to supporting the Department in carrying out such a policy of care, but there is much to be done in spreading this attitude to all the staff and, equally important, to have our residents feel that these principles are something they are of right entitled to and should expect.

3.2　It is considered that much more can be done, beyond meeting basic physical needs, to improve the residents' quality of life, even taking into account the limitations of the building. One wonders, for example, how many staff think to knock on a resident's door before entering!

3.3   We do not yet have a prospectus for the home, but this is something that the senior staff would like to produce as soon as possible.

4.   DAILY PATTERN OF RESIDENTS' LIVES

4.1   A reasonable number of residents (approximately half) do rise and retire to bed at times of their own choice. The remainder all need assistance because of their physical frailty or mental condition and it is questionable whether they are able to exercise any real choice. We feel there are a number of points regarding this:

4.1.1   Those residents who are able to make a choice still seem to adhere to the old-fashioned attitude of early to bed and early to rise and this is difficult to change with such elderly people.

4.1.2   Our own staff work patterns and attitudes have not, in the past, been necessarily oriented towards meeting residents' needs other than those of a purely physical sort.

4.1.3   The size of the home presents problems, not only on account of the design, but because the sheer number of residents does demand a heavy emphasis on physical work such as bathing, dressing and toileting, thereby using up the bulk of available staff time.

4.1.4   The deployment of the staff is probably not as efficient as it could be with some imbalance between morning and afternoon/evening.

4.2   Educational, recreational and voluntary activities: there is no clearly displayed programme of activities and no notice board which could be used for this purpose. There is, in fact, no properly planned daily or weekly programme of activities and this is just one of the many areas that the Head of Home wants to tackle as soon as possible. We are arranging for the handyman to install a notice board. At present the activities are as follows:

4.2.1   Approximately 20 residents have daily newspapers and magazines.

4.2.2   Two residents have their own televisions and several have their own radios.

4.2.3   We have a small library of large print books and these are changed periodically by the library.

4.2.4   Occasional outings, but very few.

4.2.5   Hairdressing for two sessions per week, but these are not really sufficient.

4.2.6   A weekly occupational therapy session, attended by approximately six residents. One resident, Mr. Cole, who is a double amputee, spends most of his time making lamps, ash-trays, trays and pot-stands.

4.2.7   The WRVS come in weekly and provide a shop/trolley.

4.2.8   Three students from the local school come in on a voluntary basis every Thursday afternoon to talk to residents.

4.2.9   A church service is held every Sunday evening when eight to ten members of the local church come in and also spend time with the residents.

4.2.10   Occasional bingo sessions.

4.2.11   An organisation called Contact visits one of our residents and takes her out for trips and tea. We are hoping to develop this further, involving other residents.

4.2.12   Naomi Sinclair comes on a voluntary basis three days per week and undertakes a range of activities with residents, particularly painting.

4.2.13   A clothing shop comes twice a year.

4.3   A small number of residents are active enough to keep up outside interests and one resident attends Morgan Lodge Adult Training Centre, and another the Wellington Road Day Centre.

4.4   There is no one member of staff with a special responsibility for voluntary/social activities and it is fair to say that this is a neglected area of work.

4.5   All residents spend most of the day out of their bedrooms and, in fact, find it difficult to spend more time in their rooms, because of the geography of the building and the distance between lounges and bedrooms.

4.5.1   Only six residents have single rooms and they are the only ones who can enjoy any real form of privacy. Residents in the two- and four-bedded rooms are at a disadvantage in this respect, and the design of the communal bathrooms and toilets does not allow for privacy elsewhere.

4.5.2   We have two large lounges near the dining room and one on the first floor overlooking the front entrance. There are no other rooms other than bedrooms where residents can entertain relatives and friends.

4.6   Those residents who are able are encouraged to be independent in terms of self-care, bed-making and the upkeep of their rooms. Other, less mobile residents are encouraged to walk, dress and toilet themselves. We have had several recent successes where residents have returned from hospital in very poor condition and are now walking on their own or with minimal assistance.

4.6.1   The lack of facilities makes it difficult for individual residents to make tea, wash up and so on. Four or five residents carry out tasks around the home and a number help one another. We feel that with the right sort of encouragement more residents could be involved in this way.

4.7   All residents have some link with the community, but for a small number this is minimal. The degree of involvement outside the home varies depending on the frequency of visits from relatives and friends.

4.7.1   More can certainly be done in this direction and this highlights the need to introduce as quickly as possible proper case reviews leading to the development of individual care programmes.

5.   THE PHYSICAL CONDITIONS IN WHICH RESIDENTS LIVE

5.1 As noted, the design, furnishings and facilities of the home are not domestic in nature and do not enable very much in the way of small group activity or individual privacy.

5.2 Each resident does have his or her own possessions, but these tend to be smaller items such as photographs or ornaments. A lack of space prevents very much more than this other than perhaps a small armchair, foot-stool or a small chest of drawers. Residents would be encouraged to bring such items, and to hang pictures and to have pot plants.

5.2.1 Those residents who come to us from hospital have invariably already lost most of their possessions.

5.3 Most of the home has a comfortable temperature range, but we do have problems in the dining room, large lounge and some bedrooms. In very cold weather the temperatures are not adequate and there is a draught problem. The matter has been taken up with the Architect's Department, but so far little has been done.

5.4 As in one or two other homes the men and women use separate lounges and however hard staff have tried in the past it has been almost impossible to introduce a normal mixing of the sexes. It seems to be the men rather than the women who prefer to keep their own company.

6.   THE PROVISION OF INDIVIDUAL PROGRAMMES OF CARE, THERAPY AND TREATMENT

6.1 As mentioned earlier, there is no clearly written plan for individual residents, but we are in the process of planning case reviews with the local Area Officer, and each resident is to be sounded out about his wishes, feelings, likes and dislikes. We would also like to introduce a key worker concept, and the Head of Home is going to bring this up at the next staff meeting.

6.1.1 Dr Smith is the visiting medical officer and has 26 of the residents on his register. Altogether we deal with eight different health centres and nearly 20 general practitioners.

6.1.2 As far as we can see no formal review of drugs is carried out. This is an area to pursue with Dr Smith and the general practitioners.

6.1.3 District nurses call regularly from the practices to which they are attached.

6.1.4 We have a weekly visit from the physiotherapist for a half-day session. The Head of Home is to have a word with her about developing a physiotherapy club and also hopes to clarify her role in assessing the needs of individual residents.

6.1.5 We have not had a chiropody visit for some four months and anybody needing urgent attention would have to attend a local health centre. This arrangement is very unsatisfactory, and enquiries are being made about obtaining the services of a chiropodist on a regular basis.

6.1.6 We have a weekly half-day session from the occupational therapist and again the Head of Home is going to clarify the lady's role, especially regarding the assessment of the needs of individual residents.

6.2   Support from the area office: contact with the area office has improved since the new area manager took up his appointment and we are starting to plan proper reviews with him. We would, however, make the following comments:

6.2.1   We do not receive information regarding short stay residents until the Wednesday or Thursday prior to admission on the Saturday.

6.2.2   The information given on the request-for-admission form does not always prove to be accurate and insufficient background information is given.

6.2.3   Where appropriate, the staff would like to see more follow-up visits from fieldwork staff after admission.

6.2.4   There needs to be a better understanding of each other's work by field social workers and residential staff, and closer links with the area office. We could do more on our own part to achieve this.

6.2.5   Better arrangements should be made for senior staff, and care assistants where appropriate, to attend allocation meetings at the area office.

6.3   Residents' physical condition: 26 of the 58 residents are totally dependent on staff support, either because of the extent of their physical frailty or their mental confusion or both. Many of these residents are doubly incontinent and demand a high degree of staff time.

6.3.1   The remainder require varying degrees of support and approximately 20 residents manage with minimal support.

6.3.2   We have one man who is wheelchair independent. The rest of the residents who use wheelchairs do so because of the fluctuation in their physical state or because of the lack of staff time available. A number of residents would take as much as half- to three-quarters of an hour to walk, with staff support and sometimes two, from their rooms to living areas or vice versa. Some would never manage even with staff help.

6.3.3   We have one registered blind resident and one registered partially-sighted resident. Visits from the local Association for the Blind were made, but these have lapsed as long ago as three years.

6.3.4   While a number of residents have varying degrees of confusion, only two present any form of management problems.

6.3.5   Over the last two or three years there has been a marked deterioration in the fitness of residents on admission. Coupled with the gradual deterioration of residents who have been here for several years, this has meant that staff time is virtually wholly devoted to physical care tasks.

7. THE PROVISION OF SPECIAL MEALS AND DIETS

7.1   We feel that while residents are well fed and special diets are provided, on the whole some improvements could be made in terms of choice and variety of menu. The Head of Home is undertaking the introduction of a choice of food at mealtimes and a staggered mealtime arrangement.

7.2   The contractual supply arrangement is not a good one with frequent difficulties being experienced in terms of delivery, choice and quality. It is no exaggeration to say that some of the meat received is well below standard and this applies to fruit and vegetables as well. The bulk supply arrangements mean limitations in choice, size and brand, and the strong feeling of the staff is that we could do far better using local tradesmen.

8.   CLOTHING

8.1   Every resident has his own wardrobe and supply of marked personal clothing. The home does keep a reasonable supply of clothing for people who need extra because of incontinence or other emergencies, but once allocated these are kept by the individual. Generally we try and encourage people to spend their own money on new clothing and the staff make every effort to involve the residents' relatives in this where necessary.

8.2   Other than some of the confused residents' methods of dressing no resident is incompletely or inappropriately dressed. Residents who are fit enough are encouraged to go out to the shops to purchase clothing either with staff or relatives. Staff or relatives will shop for those unable to do so and a mobile clothing shop visits twice a year.

9.   RESIDENTS' COMMITTEES

9.1   We do not have a residents' committee at present, but this is something the Head of Home wishes to establish as soon as possible.

10.   STAFFING

10.1   Care staff: we have 430 hours for day care staff and 140 for night staff. This would appear to be right given that (a) we are able to continue using relief staff to cover holidays and sickness; and (b) we are able to carry out some adjustment to day care staff hours to enable a more satisfactory deployment of the staff, and redress some of the imbalance between morning and afternoon/evening.

10.1.1   There are still some members of staff who have rigid patterns of work and these seem to be geared to their own needs rather than the home's. Until the deployment is corrected it is difficult to say for certain that the establishment is sufficient.

10.1.2   Recruitment on the whole has not been difficult because of the local redundancies, but we find that people want to do set hours to suit themselves or that candidates are not suitable for the work. We feel a care officer structure would be a far more realistic way of recruiting the right people to follow a career in the work.

10.2   Night care staff: we feel that the size of the home warrants serious consideration for a third member of night duty staff as at 17 Craven Way and 24 The Oval, both homes for the elderly of similar size.

10.3   Domestic – general: we have 80 hours per week and find this is not sufficient as this allocation allows for no cleaning staff at weekends. 17 Craven Way, a 60-bedded home, has 105 hours, 24 The Oval 115, and some of the 40-bedded homes have 85.

10.3.1   Bearing in mind the size and age of the home we feel this should be urgently reviewed. Recruitment is not difficult although we do not have many vacancies arise.

10.4   Laundry: we have 20 hours allocated and feel that this is insufficient. We are sending sheets out for laundering to ensure that personal clothing receives adequate attention. Again, an urgent survey should be carried out.

10.5   Catering: we have 165 hours allocated on the establishment. At present these are used as follows:

Cook	42 hours
Assistant Cook	18 hours
Kitchen Domestic	76 hours

The balance of 29 hours is used to supplement the general cleaning and laundry.

10.6   Gardening: we have a visit once per week for a full day and this seems sufficient to keep the grounds tidy.

10.7   Handyman services: this is just about adequate as long as a regular weekly visit is being made.

10.8   Staff development and training: it is fair to say that this area of work has been neglected in the past although we have tried to put on occasional training programmes for the care staff. Not enough emphasis has been placed on staff development, although it is important to note that the large majority of our staff have no real interest in furthering their careers. They are largely part-time workers, housewives with family commitments. We feel that a care officer structure would eventually lead to a staff group with a more professional outlook on the work.

10.8.1   At present we have one of our young full-time care assistants on the in-service training course and we feel that she has some potential in the work.

10.9   Staff morale: the home has gone through a period of unrest and change over the last two years, and the new Head of Home has come in at a difficult time. However, with the support of the senior staff there seems to be higher morale now. The feeling is that staff are keen to work well and were previously lacking in proper direction and encouragement.

10.10   Communications: staff meetings have been infrequent, approximately every three to four months. A day report book is used for written communications and senior staff carry out formal handovers on duty in the morning and evening. The Head of Home has had one staff meeting since she came three months ago and would like to establish monthly meetings.

10.11   Senior staff: at present there are no formal weekly meetings, but this is something to be aimed for with proper records kept.

10.11.1   We have undergone a period of change for senior staff simply by the introduction of a new Head of Home who has some different ideas about management. One area of change already brought about has been the senior staff working rota. This has been altered from a system of working one long weekend in three to a two weekend on and one weekend off system where the main principle is an eight-hour day as far as this is possible. The new arrangement has caused some anxiety for Mrs Johnson and Mrs Reeves, but we hope to introduce an alternative weekend arrangement by recruiting a care assistant with special responsibilities. We have advertised and are in the process of seeing applicants. Unfortunately, the response has not been good.

11.   RECOMMENDATIONS
   (i) Urgent review of the design of the building and its facilities.
  (ii) Review of staff patterns of working together with the introduction of a key worker concept.
 (iii) Review of domestic staff establishment by work study team.
 (iv) Introduce a care officer structure as soon as possible.
  (v) Establish a frequent review system within the home to supplement the area office reviews.
 (vi) Introduce a fourth senior officer.
(vii) Establish regular staff meetings for senior staff and all staff.
(viii) Establish better links with the area office.

At the home review previously mentioned, the Director of Social Services used the Homes Manager's report as the basis for discussion. This was undoubtedly a home experiencing difficulties in a number of areas, but the new head of home was eager to bring about change, and the *identification* of the problems being faced by staff and residents was the first step in the four-stage process described earlier. This was continued in the home review as additional concerns were expressed about the facilities provided for the residents and about the quality of life they experienced, for instance noting that they had no individual lights over their beds, no locks on their bedroom doors, and no drawers with locks in their bedroom furniture.

Executive responsibilities for change were allocated to the Head of Home, the Homes Manager, the Staff Development Officer and the Assistant Director (Residential Services), with suggested time limits for the work to be accomplished.

A number of policy and practice issues came under the second heading in the change process, *realignment* or *replacement*. In some cases, merely to have identified with some formality the areas for improvement gave the impetus for action: installing a notice board; providing tea-making facilities in the lounge; appointing a member of staff as co-ordinator for voluntary work with responsibility for liaison with the volunteer organiser in the local area office; re-establishing communication with the local Association for the Blind; ensuring an increase in the amount of information being made available about residents prior to admission; setting up a residents' committee; providing a full choice of meals on a staggered basis; taking up the complaints regarding contract supplies; seeking advice from the fire officer about the need or otherwise to increase the number of night staff; looking at ways of deploying staff to better advantage; thinking in greater detail about the provision of aids for daily living; and establishing regular weekly senior staff meetings, and full staff meetings at least once a month, with minutes kept.

Other matters required a longer time span, say six months, but were given varying degrees of urgency for investigation: improving the heating in some . rooms; introducing a regular review of residents' drugs; drawing up a prospectus for the home; finding out about the possible use of electric wheelchairs; looking at the work of the occupational therapist, the physiotherapist and the chiropidist (when appointed) to make sure that maximum use was being made of their services; thinking about ways of obtaining extra financial support for the purchase of clothing and aids for residents who were incontinent; and setting up a review system for individual residents in co-operation with fieldwork staff, this being part of the plan for strengthening relationships with the area office.

Structural alterations, for example, room dividers, providing more storage space, adding a toilet in the downstairs bathroom, converting a four-bedded room into a lounge and making some of the remaining large bedrooms into two doubles, necessitated the co-operation of other departments in the local authority and entailed delays.

Although a much longer process, taking until the next review and beyond, staff training started moving the home into an exciting new *developmental* phase almost immediately, with all the attitude changes that this calls for. This is probably the most difficult part to achieve, demanding as it does a major shift in the perspectives of the staff. In a series of meetings following the review staff were helped to identify practices working against the best interests of the residents, for example, being fixated on deadlines for completing some of the routine work; spending too much time on medical dressings when the policy of the department clearly encourages the maximum involvement of district nurses; cleaning lockers for residents instead of with them; and riding people in wheelchairs instead of walking with them just to save time.

What became clear in discussion with the staff of the home was their ignorance of alternative ways of working. Previously they had had no models. Given an opportunity to express themselves they became enthusiastic about the idea of grouping the residents within the home; keen to think about the problems that this would present for individual residents; and committed to the idea of spending more time talking with residents, all of which led one staff member to exclaim spontaneously: 'We'll need to know more about relationships'.

This is not an unusual home. Others up and down the country contend with even greater difficulties, and it is important always to start 'where the home is', identifying and accepting with honesty and not dismay the geographical and organisational limitations of the home and the current personal and professional developmental levels of the staff. The home review at 49 Bridge Walk enabled staff to grow through their involvement in the exercise. They began to talk constructively about the residents and their needs, and to focus less on routines.

The Staff Development Officer described beautifully a later visit to 49 Bridge Walk: two members of staff were engaged in conversation with a resident while sitting quite relaxed on the arm of her chair. Communication of that order is experienced and not taught.

At the time of the next review some of the difficulties will remain. Others, however, will have been overcome. It will be easy to identify where there has been progress when this later *evaluation* is made. Much depends upon the energy, skill and motivation of the senior staff, both internal and external. I am convinced that without the review exercise progress would have been slower. It provided a vehicle for change.

6 The Promise of the Future

Social services departments will be responding to the needs of individuals at risk and to the needs of society for protection against its most non-conforming members until well beyond the turn of the century. Part of this response will be the provision of residential homes and schools.

While local authorities will continue to make considerable and perhaps increasing use of the private and voluntary sector, I see no reason for this to be an excuse either for reducing the residential services provided by social services departments or for giving up the struggles of recent years to improve the quality of care in the homes and schools we do provide. A great deal of progress has been made and these are now our establishments, available as community-based resources for our children, our elderly citizens and our handicapped people, and open to development in any way we choose. They are ours to shape and redesign.

Our knowledge, our intuition and much of our research evidence indicate that many present approaches are by any criteria expensive financially and emotionally, offering poor returns for our money and efforts. As suggested in Chapter 3, we have only to examine the number of children in care who become parents of children in care to establish this.

Locally based establishments

In that chapter I considered particularly the social work task with individual residents. To my mind this task is best undertaken in a person's local community, helping him or her to build upon existing affectional bonds with people and places; and to regain *in situ* personal status and self-esteem. Residential establishments must therefore become 'community homes' in the true sense. While we may accept this intellectually and theoretically, it frequently bears little relation to what happens in practice. An elderly widower moving into a residential home five miles from his friends, his favourite pub and his one remaining niece may sometimes feel more than a hundred miles away from all that contributes towards his identity and security.

Although a former approved school situated at some distance from the urban setting from which it draws its residents can hardly

...ribed as a 'community home' in the sense that I am using it,
...term is exciting in its potential as a generic concept throughout
the range of client groups. 'Community homes for adults' are as
acceptable as descriptions of units in which a number of older
people live together as are 'community homes for children'. The
fact that in the case of community homes for adults the residents
are mentally or physically handicapped, mentally ill or elderly is a
secondary consideration.

Both for children and adults, most homes should therefore be
locally based, limited in the number of residents able to live there
and developed as an acknowledged resource: for individuals, by
individuals, for the community and by the community. The
practical implementation of such a concept means moving
mountains of prejudice and layers of stigma, minimising administrative procedures and making assisted living and group living in
residential settings more palatable aspects of welfare provision, and
rights to be exercised and enjoyed in times of need.

The need for smaller units

We must move away from large institutions. Even those broken
down into smaller units are an uneasy compromise, with management functions, administrative controls and unit costs uppermost
in the minds of the power holders and decision makers. Alternatives to family life for those who need special provision can, with
few exceptions, be responded to by two alternatives: group living
units and assisted living units. Some homes are thus exclusively
concerned with group living, others are developed on the lines of
sheltered care, with a number providing a mixture, for example for
older adolescents who need a period of semi-independence before
moving on, or for elderly or handicapped people faced at a later
date with deteriorating physical or mental conditions.

For group living I take as my ideal unit size accommodation for
12 people, sometimes further broken down into two groups of six,
or even three groups of four. Within this framework there is room
for flexibility of groupings and the opportunity to change the
purpose of the home and the resident group as the needs of an area
and a community vary over time.

Redefining roles, relationships and responsibilities

Organisationally the establishment must be seen and felt as a home
by the residents and by the local community. This is the only satisfactory way forward. Staffing requirements will be determined by

the composition, special needs and behaviour difficulties of client group, with increased autonomy in terms of budget control and case accountability passing either to the head of the home or to the staff group as a whole. I would maintain that the structures we have created of officer in charge, deputy officer in charge, third in charge, group leader, deputy group leader and so on will more and more be experienced as unhelpful and outmoded management devices preventing extensions of thought and practice in living and working with people in groups. By the turn of the century residents will no longer be prepared to accept the subservient client role and the hierarchy of management at present found in some homes. Staff too, through training, personal development, political awareness and their membership of a more classless society will reject for themselves and on behalf of their residents the cumbersome structures that we have built. We must prepare for that time.

A key person in the development of homes will be the consultant, working with staff, sometimes with residents, sometimes with staff and residents. An expert in human development and group dynamics, he or she will not be concerned with furniture and fittings, and will not manage the home, but act as a sub-station from which will flow the power to analyse, to understand, to clarify, to plan and to enable.

The first-level management of a home seems best served by a small committee made up of social services department staff, members, residential social work staff, residents, residents' families and people from the local community, say, a group of seven electing their own chairperson. This may be one way of shifting power from the present impenetrable hierarchies to the individuals and communities for whom the homes exist. For too long and with only minimal results we have operated a daddy-knows-best policy in the control and management of people and homes. I cannot believe that universal progress on the lines I have described is now possible within this policy.

The day-to-day control of homes by centrally-based management should become loose, with accountability becoming noticeably apparent at the annual or biennial in-depth reviews of establishments designed to look at the work of a home or school from every possible point of view, as discussed in Chapter 5 and set out in the Appendix. We must trust staff more. If they are not trusted, they will be less able to trust residents.

Towards the 21st century

As we approach the 21st century many of the power struggles enacted in the wider society will be re-enacted within residential settings: residents will not so easily accept control without explanation; they will expect to be involved in decision making; and there will be automatic rights of appeal if they feel aggrieved. Within staff groups, many battles have yet to be fought between the 'old guard' and the 'new guard'.

Alvin Toffler's book, *The Third Wave*, is helpful as we embark on our journey into the future. The author suggests that we are now experiencing the impact of the third tidal wave of change in history, the first being the agricultural revolution and the second the industrial revolution.[1]

Toffler sees the third wave as a challenge to the power élites in both capitalist and socialist societies with the collision between the defenders of second-wave civilisation and the advocates of the third wave becoming the single most important political confrontation of our time. He continues:

> A new civilisation is emerging in our lives, and blind men everywhere are trying to suppress it. This new civilisation brings with it new family styles; changed ways of working, loving and living; a new economy; new political conflicts; and beyond all this an altered consciousness as well ... Millions are already attuning their lives to the rhythms of tomorrow. Others, terrified of the future, are engaged in a desperate, futile flight into the past and are trying to restore the dying world that gave them birth.[2]

Tory party strategies are definitely second-wave, with many residential staff trapped within policies, procedures, financial constraints and local political controls that make the task of attuning residents' lives to the rhythms of tomorrow even more difficult. In the third-wave civilisation, in residential work as in other spheres of human activity, the philosophy is no longer 'more of the same' as we respond to residents' needs. As Toffler indicates,[3] tomorrow is not merely an extension of today with trends continuing in linear fashion. At some points in our history new phenomena have to be addressed. Within residential care I feel that we have reached such a point.

Residential care in a new society

In the final paragraphs of this short volume I invite readers to think about these new phenomena and the resultant redefinition of residential social work. This may well mean conflict, both with the forces seeking to squash into the ground the underprivileged and the unwanted, and with colleagues content to perpetuate second-wave factory-type practices.

I see four major thrusts for practitioners over the next two decades: to harass and weaken by all legitimate means, either as individuals or collectively, any political manoeuvre which prevents residents from retaining and increasing appropriate independence of decision making and action; to 'name' assertively any act, policy, programme or plan that compounds the low status of residents and contributes towards the cumulative social injustice that they bear; to eradicate from our establishments the vestiges of bad practice; and, while not ignoring the general issues, to resolve to maximise on each possible occasion the good that evolves from a skilled and concerned response to the 'particular', so aptly referred to by William Blake in his epic poem *Jerusalem*.

There is little to say about the need for political action. At the moment too much smacks of punishment and control with the freedom of some residents stifled by prejudice and power struggles. The 'professional' part of the job calls for practitioners able to engage in debate and action that arrest the erosion of the present pockets of good practice – often large pockets – and improve the quality of life for residents. They need also to attack housing, education, employment and penal policies directly responsible for the eventual admission of people to residential settings. *For staff unthinkingly to translate environmental conditions into widespread individual and family pathology is to intensify the injustices to which residents have already been subjected.*

Secondly, I appreciate very much the increasing occurrences of 'giving a name' to practices causing personal discomfort to the practitioner. Many people are now skilled and determined in this, persuasively stating their point in respect of a poorly planned admission, an unfair report or a badly conducted case conference. People with courage to speak out either to residential colleagues or to fieldwork staff may experience loneliness and fear rejection in the short term. The later rewards are great because there is always respect for opinions focused exclusively on finding better ways of working with residents.

The third point relates to improving practice within our own establishments. We really do have to put our house in order. Compounding the low status of residents and humiliating them in the ways I described in Chapter 1 are reminders of the distance still to be travelled.

My last point also relates to practice and draws on a line from Blake's *Jerusalem*: 'He who would do good to another must do it in Minute Particulars'. This plea to respond to residents in 'minutely organised particulars' is central to our work. It is often the small act, the thoughtful gesture, the brief, warm exchange that creates the climate for purposeful living in groups.

I look optimistically towards the future. As we seek to clarify and to implement the social work task in residential settings as our response to those unable to live independently in their own homes, so our notion of progress will be based on different criteria. Gradually new ways of living and working together will emerge which are more helpful to residents and more rewarding for staff. While it may not be possible to keep pace with the revolutionary vision of Toffler, I am certain that whatever developments occur in residential care we are unlikely to return to the 'naïve, unilinear, Pollyannaish progressivism'[4] that characterised our thinking for so many years.

Appendix

A framework for review

The following framework is by no means complete. It does, however, suggest practice areas common to many establishments and provides detailed questions designed to put under scrutiny the level of service offered to residents. Many topics lend themselves to adaptation and expansion according to the particular aims and objectives of individual homes. Residential schools, too, will find a great deal of direct relevance to their work. The checklist may have a number of uses: as a method of self-assessment; as preparation for a formal review; or as a basis for the review itself.

1. Simple statistics
Number of admissions and discharges;
Facts about residents who have been admitted;
Facts about residents who have been discharged;
Number of staff resignations;
Reasons for staff resignations;
Number of new staff;
Number of rota visits by members;
Number of staff who have been able to take advantage of some form of training. Indicate the type of training: Certificate of Qualification in Social Work? Certificate in Social Service? In-service training? Short courses?
Amount of sick leave;
Intervals between the departure of staff following resignations and their replacements taking up new appointments;
Number of recorded accidents to staff;
Number of recorded accidents to residents;
Cost of furniture replacement and repairs;
Cost of repairs to the fabric of the building, for example replacing broken windows.

2. The environment
What is the general appearance of the home? Is it clean? Are the lounges comfortable? Do bedrooms and bedspaces reflect the individual tastes of the residents? Are there sufficient toilets and bathrooms? Are they clean and fresh?

Is the building in a good state of repair and decoration? Is it always warm enough? Is it well lighted? Is it attractively lighted? Are there satisfactory arrangements for ensuring that the building is kept in working order? Are there any minor works needed to improve the accommodation? Is there a programme of redecoration laid down by the local authority?

Comment on the noise level, and the kind of noise, at various times and in various places;

Are any areas associated with strong, unpleasant smells? What attempts have been made to combat these?

Are the rooms adequately furnished? Curtained? Carpeted? Are curtains cleaned regularly? Are carpets deep-cleaned at intervals? Are tablecloths used? Is the tableware home-like or canteen-like? Is the crockery chipped? Is the cutlery always clean?

What changes could be made in the environment that would improve the residents' quality of life? Can anything be done to make better use of the outside recreation or play area?

3.   Facilities and equipment

In what ways is the home well equipped? Is the best use being made of the equipment available? Are repairs put in hand promptly?

In what ways is the home poorly equipped? Can these deficiencies be made good?

What additional facilities would improve the work it is possible to do with residents?

Are there additional transport requirements? On what basis would you justify these?

4   Safety

Is the fire equipment always in order?

Are fire drills held regularly? Is a record kept of these?

Are the staff fully conversant with their responsibilities in the event of an outbreak of fire?

Has the officer in charge of the local fire station visited the home? Has an invitation been extended to his crews to make themselves familiar with the layout of the building?

Are regulations regarding furniture in corridors and the closing of fire doors strictly observed?

Do staff have some knowledge of first aid?

Do they know emergency procedures in case of sudden illness or accident?

Are they able to identify the effects of excessive drug taking?
Glue sniffing?
Is electrical equipment tested regularly? In the case of young
children, handicapped people and elderly residents, are
additional precautions taken as a guard against inquisitiveness, a
lack of dexterity, failing eyesight or an unsteady gait?
When was the electrical wiring in the building last tested?
Have the driving licences of all staff members who take residents
in their cars or drive local authority vehicles been checked? Is
there a lower age limit for staff members acting as drivers? When
staff are driving their own cars is a declaration made that they
are comprehensively insured with a special clause on the policy
relating to the carriage of residents? Is there a local authority
driving test to be taken in addition to that required by law?
Have the drivers on the staff taken this extra test before driving
residents in local authority vehicles?
Are any substances, for example pills or bleach, easily accessible
to residents who by reason of age or mental condition might use
them in a way which would put them at risk?
Are small bottles of cleaning fluids filled from large containers
always clearly marked?

5. Staff

Is an induction programme worked out for each new member of
staff?
What arrangements are made for applicants for posts to acquaint
themselves with the home prior to interview?
How are the residents prepared for the arrival of a new member
of staff?
How are ancillary staff consulted about decisions affecting them
and their work? To whom are they responsible? Who is
concerned with developing their skills and reviewing their
relationships within the home?
Are there any expectations about staff and smoking? In the
kitchen? In the dining-room? In residents' bedrooms? On duty?
Are there different rules for residents?
What problems arise when staff are on sick leave? In what way is
the standard of care affected?

6. Support and supervision

What do staff members understand by support?

Has regular supervision been introduced? Is this on an individual
or a group basis?
If individual supervision has been established, is it available to
all members of the care staff? Is it regular?
Do the staff value supervision? How is this known?
Is an external consultant working with the home? How does he
or she approach the task? Is this meeting the needs of the staff?
To what extent is the homes officer able to combine the
managerial, educational, advisory and supportive elements of the
post? If his or her approach is not completely successful is there
a way of suggesting that there should be a change of emphasis?
Are there regular meetings with all staff members, or only
between the head of home and the deputy?

7.   Internal management

Do staff know who is responsible for making up the duty rota?
Are they included in the process? Is the basis of the rota the
needs of the residents or the needs of the staff?
Are staff certain of having two days off together each week if
that be their wish? If not, is an alternative arrangement with
their agreement?
Under what circumstances would they be asked to work split
duties?
Who is responsible for authorising overtime?
Does the staffing establishment allow sufficiently for periods of
sick leave? A greater concentration of staff during school
holidays? Have any changes occurred which might affect the
staffing establishment?
Is the rota always worked out to allow for an overlap of staff
going off duty and those coming on duty so that they are able to
pass on information in person?
Is the maximum use being made of part-time staff? Are they
included in all the activities of the home whenever possible?
Do residents always know who is going to look after them? Do
they know who will be sleeping in the building each night?

8.   Communication and decision making

Do residents know what records are kept about them? Are the
reports on the files shared with them? How is it possible to
justify keeping the contents of the file from residents?
Do staff receive special help in writing reports? Are reports
going outside the home always the result of collective opinion

and never the work of just one member of staff? What steps are
taken to separate fact, opinion and speculation?
Do residents know when meetings about them are taking place,
for example, case conferences and reviews? Would it be possible
for them to be further involved in the process? What prevents
full participation? Are there adequate opportunities for all
members of staff to express their views?
What steps do senior staff take at an informal level to keep in
touch with the views and aspirations of their colleagues?
How are the decisions communicated within the home? What
methods are used for making clear who is responsible for seeing
that decisions are carried out? How are the effects of decisions
reviewed?
What part do residents play in the consultation process? How
might this be improved?
Who controls day-to-day expenditure, for example the use of the
petty cash? Are the present arrangements satisfactory?

9. Residents
How are residents welcomed to the home? How are residents
prepared for a newcomer to the group?
Praise, rewards and sanctions – what methods are used and why?
Are any improvements feasible?
What opportunities are given for the development of initiative
and responsibility?
In considering the needs and interests of individual children and
supporting the work of the school what special provision is there
for gifted children? Children who are slow to learn? Children for
whom English is a second language? Children who have a
specific skill or talent? Is the home able to respond to these
varying demands?
Do residents feel that their personal belongings are treated with
respect? What steps are taken to safeguard their possessions?
How often do they complain about damage or theft? What are
the staff responses to any such complaints?
Is the menu available in advance? Whenever possible, are
residents involved in planning the menus? Is there always a
choice of dishes at mealtimes? Are special diets catered for,
offering the maximum variety of food and drink?
Is every resident appropriately placed in the home? If not, is
every effort being made to find the right alternative?

10.   *Medical*

What is the level of sickness among residents? Is there any pattern of illness?

Who prescribes treatment for minor ills? Who decides that the services of a medical practitioner are necessary? On what basis?

Are local practitioners or the medical officer to the home responsive to the residents and their needs for medical treatment? Do they express satisfaction with the treatment they receive?

Do residents have any choice of medical practitioners?

Who hands out pills and medicines? Are these kept under lock and key? Do all members of staff have access to pills and medicines? Do students have similar access?

Is a record kept of the drugs, pills and medicines to be found in the home? Of the occasions when they are given to residents?

Who is responsible for destroying the pills remaining from an unfinished course of treatment? Is medicine that has been prescribed for one resident ever given to another? Under what circumstances? Who would decide to do this?

In the case of residents under 16, are all members of staff aware of the procedures necessary for giving permission for surgical treatment?

When a resident is in hospital, is regular visiting maintained from the home?

Is contraceptive advice freely available for all who need it, including those under 16 years of age?

11.   *Family, relatives and friends*

Is the reception of visitors by staff courteous and helpful, especially for unscheduled visits?

As far as possible, are arrangements made for a member of staff always to meet with parents or relatives on their first visit to the home?

From outside the establishment, how do telephone callers perceive your home? Are the lines always engaged, making it difficult to get through, especially for people using a call-box? Is every effort made to answer telephone callers' queries or to respond to their problems? Are internal connections picked up, or are callers left not knowing whether they have been forgotten? Is there a telephone for the exclusive use of residents? Are they able to make their calls in private?

For first-time visitors to the home, are clear directions

available, preferably in written form? Do these directions include a map showing the location of the home?

Are attempts made to give a resident's family or relatives an understanding of what the home is trying to do? Is a prospectus available?

Has thought been given to the language used in writing to parents or relatives?

How are complaints or difficulties dealt with?

What opportunities are there for parents or relatives and residents to meet with a member of staff (a) as a matter of routine or (b) at their own or the home's request?

12.   Community links

List the most important links with the local community.

Are residents involved in the community to the maximum extent possible? If not, what prevents this?

Who is responsible for developing links with the neighbourhood?

Is any use made of volunteers? How might their involvement be improved?

13.   Training and development

Describe your contacts with the training section.

Has the responsible training officer visited your home during the last year? Have the training needs of the staff been discussed with him or her? Do members of staff know the person to contact if they wish to discuss their individual expectations for training?

14.   Students

Do students know who is responsible for them? Are messages conveyed to students about what is expected of them?

Do they always know well in advance when they will be off duty? Whether study time is included in their working week? Which meetings they should attend? What documentation they have access to? What written reports they should produce?

Do all requests for student placements come from the training officer? What criteria are used for deciding to accept or not to accept a student on placement? Is the staff group involved in this decision? On what basis is a supervisor appointed? Is regular supervision given? Are time and space created for a supervisor to undertake work unhurriedly and in a relaxed atmosphere? Are uninterrupted supervision sessions guaranteed?

Similar series of questions could, for example, be framed in respect of the admission of residents, the social work task (see Chapter 3), school and work, the conduct of reviews on individual residents, and relationships with fieldworkers.

If the review is used *as a self-assessment*, there are yet more questions for *the individual staff member to ask him or herself*: Am I reliable? Do I make plans and anticipate the needs of residents? Do I spend sufficient time talking with residents? What efforts do I make to know better those residents who do not make obvious demands on me? Do I take account of individual differences among residents in my relationships with them and in making provision for them? In what ways do I try to ensure continuity between my work and what occurs before and after? How do I contribute to the development of good relationships with residents, colleagues, residents' relatives, residents' friends and other people connected with the home or school? Do I participate in the discussion at staff meetings?

Then, of course, members of staff must face up to the acid test in any process of evaluation:

Would I recommend a friend to apply for a post in this home or school?

How would I feel about a friend or relative of mine living here as a resident?

How would I feel about being a resident in this home or school?

Notes and References

Chapter 1

1. Letters page, *Community Care*, 27 November 1980, p. 9
2. Reported in the *Daily Mirror*, 4 November 1980, p. 3

Chapter 2

1. Department of Education and Science, 1980, *Community Homes with Education*, HMI Series: Matters for Discussion 10, London, HMSO
2. *Special Educational Needs,* 1978, Report of the Committee of Enquiry into the Education of Handicapped Children and Young People, London, HMSO, Cmnd. 3703
3. A theme developed by Dr Spyros Doxiadis, President, Institute of Child Health, and Minister of Social Services, Greece, at the 31st Annual Lecture of the CIBA Foundation, 1979
4. Gibran, K. 1971 (first published 1926), *The Prophet,* London, William Heinemann
5. Shaw, G. B. 1946 (first published 1903), 'The revolutionist's handbook' in *Man and Superman*, Harmondsworth, Penguin Books, pp. 281–2
6. Developed from a comment by Cravioto, J. 1979, in 'The child and the environment', *The Child in the World of Tomorrow*, Oxford, Pergamon Press, p. 432
7. Holt, J. 1975, *Escape from Childhood*, Harmondsworth, Pelican Books, p. 66; © John Holt, 1974. Reprinted by permission of Penguin Books Ltd.

Chapter 3

1. Adapted, with kind permission, from Dockar-Drysdale, B. 1973, *Consultation in Child Care*, London, Longman, pp. 134–6
2. McCullers, C. 1962 (first published in the USA, 1946), *The Member of the Wedding*, Harmondsworth, Penguin Books, pp. 7 and 52
3. Pirsig, R. M. (1976) (first published 1974), *Zen and the Art of Motor Cycle Maintenance*, London, Corgi Books, p. 60
4. Ward, L. 1977, 'Clarifying the residential social work task', *Social Work Today*, vol. 9, no. 2, p. 21
5. Davis, L. F. 1975, '285 children in care: an evaluation', *The Community Home Schools Gazette*, vol. 69, no. 6, p. 290

Chapter 4

1. Arnold, M. B. 1960, *Emotion and Personality*, vol. 1 Psychological Aspects, New York, Columbia University Press, pp. 20–21
2. Pasternak, B. 1958, *Doctor Zhivago*, translated from the Russian by Max Hayward and Manya Harari, London, Collins and Harvil Press, p. 429
3. Laing, R. D. 1965, *The Divided Self*, Harmondsworth, Penguin Books, p. 34
4. Wright, G. 1978, 'A model of supervision for residential staff', *Social Work Today*, vol. 9, no. 45, pp. 22–3

Chapter 5

1. Personal Social Services Council, 1975, *Living and Working in Residential Homes*, a working party report, p. 12
2. Dinnage, R. and Pringle, M. K. 1967, *Residential Child Care – Facts and Fallacies*, London, Longman, p. 49
3. Prosser, H. 1976, *Perspectives on Residential Child Care*, Windsor, National Foundation for Educational Research, p. 24
4. Walton, R. 1978, 'Research for practice', *Social Work Today,* vol. 9, no. 22, p. 22
5. City of Salford, 1977, *Moorfield Observation and Assessment Centre*, a report of a committee of inquiry, p. 75
6. Irving, W. 1850, *Tales of a Traveller*, London, Bohn, p. vi

Chapter 6

1. Toffler, A. 1980, *The Third Wave*, New York, Morrow
2. Ibid, p. 25
3. Ibid, p. 145
4. Ibid, p. 312

Additional references

The following references are all to articles by L. F. Davis in *Social Work Today*:

1978, 'Beyond the key worker concept', vol. 9, no. 19
1978, 'A strategy for change', vol. 9, no. 28
1978, 'Working with adolescents', vol. 9, no. 46
1979, 'Improving practice', vol. 10, no. 31
1980, 'Dispelling the fears of the long night', vol. 11, no. 24
1980, 'Putting philosophy into practice', vol. 11, no. 36
1981, 'Embarking upon a journey into the future', vol. 12, no. 22

Index